# INQUIRY

INTO THE

# ORIGINAL LANGUAGE

OF

# ST. MATTHEW'S GOSPEL;

WITH RELATIVE DISCUSSIONS ON

## THE LANGUAGE OF PALESTINE IN THE TIME OF CHRIST,

AND ON

## THE ORIGIN OF THE GOSPELS.

BY THE

REV. ALEXANDER ROBERTS, M.A.

MINISTER OF THE PRESBYTERIAN CHURCH, ST. JOHN'S WOOD.

WIPF & STOCK · Eugene, Oregon

῾Ο οὐρανὸς καὶ ἡ γῆ παρελεύσονται, οἱ δὲ λόγοι μου οὐ μὴ παρέλθωσι.

**St. Matt. xxiv. 35; St. Mark, xiii. 31; St. Luke, xxi. 33.**

Wipf and Stock Publishers
199 W 8th Ave, Suite 3
Eugene, OR 97401

Inquiry Into the Original Language of St. Matthew's Gospel
With Relative Discussion on the Language of Palestine in the Time of Christ, and on the Origin of the Gospels.
By Roberts, Alexander
ISBN 13: 978-1-60608-920-0
Publication date 11/4/2009
Previously published by Samuel Bagster and Sons, 1859

# PREFACE.

The object of the following Treatise is to vindicate and uphold the Greek original of St. Matthew's Gospel. This has been attempted on other, and, it is hoped, more satisfactory grounds, than those which have sometimes been assigned by the advocates of that opinion; and in the partially new aspect which has thus been given to the argument, as well as in the belief that such a work is at present seasonable, is to be found the special reason for this publication.

Every one at all conversant with Biblical studies, knows how keenly the question, respecting the original language of St. Matthew's Gospel, has been discussed, and how diverse are the conclusions which have been formed regarding it. The question is, indeed, one which is beset with peculiar difficulties, and which demands no ordinary patience and reflection from those who enter on its consideration. But with all its perplexities, it is a question which must be faced by every critical student of Scripture. It meets him at the very threshold of the New Testament; and he soon perceives, that it is not only first in the order in which it occurs, but first also, in many respects, in the importance which belongs to it. As will fully appear in the following pages, it is an inquiry of the very gravest practical importance. It involves in its settlement some very momentous consequences, and it requires, therefore, not only to be investigated with earnestness, but with a solemn feeling of responsibility and reverence.

The author was led by circumstances, which it is unnecessary to mention, to enter with the deepest interest into "this noble controversy."* While still a minister of the Free Church of Scotland, in a remote country town, he sought to do a little (though from want both of time and books, it could then only be very little) at critical pursuits; and when, in the Providence of God, removed, some time ago, to a charge in connexion with the sister Church in England, it was one of the most highly-prized advantages of his new position, that he found his facilities for sacred study greatly increased. At the same time, he may be allowed to state, in apology for any marks of haste, or any errors of reference which may be found in the subsequent pages, that his researches have been pursued, and his work composed, in such hours of leisure as could be "redeemed" from the duties of a pastoral charge in the Metropolis.

In addition to the important question respecting St. Matthew's Gospel, the subject of the origin of the first three Gospels has also been considered. A simple, and, it is believed, satisfactory

* "Hæc nobilis controversia."—*Poli Synopsis.*

solution of that *quæstio vexata* has been proposed; and if the theory here suggested be deemed worthy of general acceptance by the learned, a very troublesome and perplexing problem will be taken out of the way of sacred criticism.

The author has very freely expressed his opinion of some works and theories which came to be referred to in the course of the discussion. This candour he deems necessary in every controversial publication; but he earnestly hopes, that, while *works* are freely criticised, there is nothing which will appear needlessly offensive to the *writers*. There ought to be the greatest liberty allowed and taken in dealing with opinions and publications; but their authors, however mistaken, are, if labouring in what they judge the service of truth, entitled to sincere respect. The protecting shield of our great Master's golden rule is thrown around every one, however humble, who seeks to advance the interests of sacred truth, and that, although his views themselves may be very erroneous, and subjected to unsparing criticism and unqualified condemnation.

The knowledge of Syriac possessed by the writer is, as yet, very slight; but sufficient, he trusts, to warrant the remarks which have been made on Dr. Cureton's Syriac Gospels. Indeed, so elaborately has that work been edited by the learned Canon, that a mere Greek scholar (assuming, as we have done, the *correctness* of his renderings) is enabled pretty easily to judge of its pretensions. The opinion expressed regarding it in this treatise is very plain and decided—perhaps it may seem unnecessarily severe; but with the author's present convictions of the real character and tendency of the work, no other, or less forcible language could have been employed respecting it.

With the assured expectation of receiving, at the hands of Biblical scholars, whatever attention and indulgence he deserves, and with the sincerest respect for those eminent critics from whose views he has so often felt it necessary to dissent, the author leaves his work to be judged of by all that are competent to express an opinion regarding it, and who take an interest in its deeply important subject.

St. John's Wood, London,
*April* 21, 1859.

# CONTENTS.

## CHAPTER I.



## CHAPTER II.

### LANGUAGE OF PALESTINE IN THE TIME OF CHRIST.



## CHAPTER III.

### INTERNAL EVIDENCE OF THE PROPER ORIGINALITY OF THE EXISTING GREEK GOSPEL OF ST. MATTHEW.

## CHAPTER IV.

### EXTERNAL EVIDENCE.



## CHAPTER V.

# INQUIRY

INTO

# THE ORIGINAL LANGUAGE OF

# ST. MATTHEW'S GOSPEL.

---

## CHAPTER I.

### STATEMENT OF THE QUESTION, AND OF THE METHOD IN WHICH THIS INQUIRY IS CONDUCTED.

THREE opinions are current among Biblical scholars, at the present day, as to the language in which the Gospel of St. Matthew was originally written.

The first of these opinions is, that St. Matthew wrote his Gospel *in Hebrew only;* that is, in the modified form of Hebrew, generally spoken of as the Aramæan or Syro-Chaldaic dialect, and which is supposed to have been the ordinary language of Palestine in the days of Christ. This opinion has been very strenuously maintained by many eminent critics, and is usually expressed by those who hold it with very great confidence. Greswell, *e. g.*, declares, that "no matter of fact which rests upon the faith of testimony can be considered certain, if this be not so;"[a] and Tregelles remarks, that, "in his judgment, *all testimony* is in favour of a Hebrew original of St. Matthew's Gospel, and of that only."[b] The holders of this hypothesis all agree, of course, in regarding our present Greek Gospel as only a version of the original; but differ widely among themselves as to the degree of authority which they are inclined to ascribe to the supposed translation. These varieties of judgment, as to the inspiration and canonical authority of the existing Gospel of St. Matthew, when

[a] Harmony of the Gospels, i. 125. [b] Horne and Tregelles, p. 420.

it is viewed as a translation from the Hebrew, will be afterwards considered: meanwhile, we may observe regarding this first opinion, that, without taking into account the ancient fathers of the church, who are in this matter to be looked at rather as witnesses than as advocates, it has been maintained in modern times by Grotius, Walton, Mill, Michaelis, Marsh, Eichhorn, Campbell, Davidson, Tregelles, Cureton, and many others, both on the continent and in our own country.

The second and counter opinion to that just stated, is, that St. Matthew wrote in *Greek only;* and that, accordingly, the work which we now possess under his name, is the veritable original. This opinion numbers, perhaps, as many and as eminent names among its defenders as does the former, although it appears, of late years, to have been losing ground. The cause of this probably has been, that many who would otherwise have felt themselves constrained to adopt and defend the true and exclusive originality of our present Greek Gospel, have deemed the third hypothesis, to be immediately mentioned, a preferable and more tenable position. There have not, however, been wanting, within a recent period, expressions of opinion as confident in favour of this second hypothesis as those which were quoted in support of the first. Thus an able writer in the Edinburgh Review (July, 1851) declares that "the casual remark of a professed anecdote-collector, whose judgment is entirely disabled by the historian who records it, is, after all, the *sole foundation* for the statement that St. Matthew wrote his Gospel in Hebrew:" and the recent editor of Diodati affirms, in his Preface, that "if the records of history and the reasonings of logic have any value, the books of the New Canon from Matthew to the Apocalypse were certainly Greek in the Apostolic autographs." Among the more celebrated defenders of this second opinion, we may name Erasmus, Calvin, Lightfoot, Wetstein, Lardner, Hales, Hug, De Wette, Credner, and Moses Stuart.

It will naturally occur to every reader, from a perusal of the above lists of eminent critics, ranged against each other in this controversy, and from the decisive way in which their different opinions have been expressed, that there must be strong arguments on both sides of this question; and that it can be no easy matter for an impartial inquirer to make choice between them. Such is, in truth, the case; and the consequence has been, as usually happens in such circumstances, that a *middle* opinion has been sought, which is thought by its supporters to absorb the conflicting evidence on both sides, and thus to furnish a means of escape from the formidable difficulties which appear to beset both the first and second hypotheses.

This third opinion is, that St. Matthew wrote his Gospel *both* in Greek and Hebrew, the two editions being either given to the world simultaneously, as some think, or rather, as more are inclined to believe, at different periods, according to the varying circumstances and necessities of the church. This hypothesis, although but of very recent origin, already numbers not a few highly respectable names among its advocates, and is at present a favourite theory, both in this country and with some able and orthodox theologians in Germany. The ground on which it rests is briefly indicated in these words of Townson: "There seems more reason for allowing two originals than for contesting either; the consent of antiquity pleading strongly for the Hebrew, and evident marks of originality for the Greek."[c] This opinion has of late years found zealous supporters on the continent in Guerike, Olshausen, and Thiersch; and in Kitto, Horne, Lee, and others in this country.[d]

It is a curious psychological problem, how so many able and learned critics, looking at this question with a sincere desire to know the truth, and with exactly the same data on which to form their judgment, should have been guided to such contradictory results. It cannot be doubted, indeed, that, in some cases, dog-

[c] Discourses on the Gospels, i. 31.

[d] Considerable confusion exists in the lists of writers usually given as holding the several hypotheses. Thus, the name of Whitby is mentioned in Horne's Introduction among the supporters both of the first and third opinions; and Olshausen is ranked by Stuart (Notes to Fosdick's Hug, p. 704) as maintaining the Hebrew original exclusively, whereas he ought to be numbered with the advocates of the third hypothesis, as above. While, as has been remarked by Dr. Tregelles, the question cannot be settled by mere names, it is desirable, if these are given at all, that they should be correctly classed under one or other of the three well-defined opinions. Our lists might have been greatly extended, but sufficient names have been given as specimens, and no catalogue could pretend to give the whole.

matic prepossessions have operated to the detriment of the critical judgment. This is sufficiently obvious from the fact, that most Romish writers have been upon the one side, and most Protestant writers on the other. The former have, for the most part, maintained the hypothesis of a Hebrew, and the latter of a Greek original; and this is but too plainly in accordance with the doctrinal leanings of their respective churches. Romanists are anxious, at all times, to magnify the authority of the church; and in this question they find an excellent opportunity for doing so, at the expense of their opponents. They eagerly adopt the opinion that our existing Gospel of St. Matthew is merely a version from the original Hebrew, executed by some unknown translator; and then they easily fix their adversaries in the dilemma either of admitting it into the canon of Scripture solely on the ground that the church has sanctioned it, or of denying that it is possessed of any authority at all. With Protestants, again, it is a fundamental principle to uphold the supreme authority of the Word of God, in opposition to all merely ecclesiastical claims upon their reverence and submission; and this they have felt no easy matter in regard to the existing Gospel of St. Matthew. In order to place it on the same footing as the other books of the New Testament, it is necessary to make out, either that the original Gospel was in fact that which we now possess, or that our present Greek is an equally inspired and authoritative work as the original Hebrew; and in grappling with the difficulties of the question, Protestant writers have sometimes been tempted to *assume* the point which they were required to *prove*, and to seek support for their position in grounds that cannot be maintained in argument.[e]

[e] Many quotations might be brought forward from the older writers on this subject, in illustration of what is stated above. Let the following suffice. We quote first from a Popish writer:—"Cum Evangelium Matthæi Hebraice sit scriptum, et vero illud hodie non extet, ideo *necessario ad divinam et infallibilem Ecclesiæ auctoritatem nobis recurrendum*, quâ negatâ nullus sit Evangelii hujus usus, cum fides interpretis sit incerta et nomen ignotum." (*Adami Contzennii* Commentaria in quatuor Evangelia, 1626.) Michaelis remarks on this, that many felt the argument very annoying (Vielen zum grossen Aergerniss), and we have a proof of it in the following words of the learned Protestant writer Flacius. He says, "Si id semel constituatur, hunc librum initio Hebraice, non Græce scriptum, et ab aliquo ignoti nominis, authoritatisve,

But after all such deductions have been made, there still remains a large number of thoroughly honest and impartial inquirers who have been led to opposite conclusions on this question, and that, in some instances, in spite of what might have been deemed their doctrinal tendencies. Thus, to give only two names, which may be regarded as representative of many more:—Hug, the celebrated Roman Catholic Professor in the University of Freyburg, is one of the most strenuous and successful defenders of the Greek original; while Tregelles, an earnest Protestant scholar among ourselves, is one of the ablest and most determined advocates of the opinion that St. Matthew wrote in Hebrew exclusively.

Leaving out of view, then, dogmatic prejudices, as far from sufficient to account for that diversity of opinion which prevails upon this subject, it appears to us that such differences may, in many cases, find their explanation in the difference of *priority and prominence* awarded by the several inquirers to the two great divisions of the evidence. It need scarcely be said that much depends, in every case of conflicting probabilities, on the method in which particular parts of the evidence are taken up and considered. One man may place the facts in such a manner, as that, while in a sense admitting them all, he will infallibly be led to a different conclusion from another man, who has considered them with equal honesty of purpose, but in a different order. And thus, as chemists now inform us, that it is the *order* in which the particles of a body are arranged, even more than their *nature*, which imparts to the substance its special properties, so, in an argument like the present, the final result which is reached will often be influenced more by the particular *method* in which the inquiry is conducted, than by the actual force of the evidence which is produced. This necessarily follows from the very great plausibility with which, as all that are well-informed upon the subject must admit, either side of the question may be argued. There are strong arguments apparently in favour of the proper originality of our existing Greek

ac etiam fidei, homine, tantâ præsertim libertate conversum esse, non parum profecto de ejus authoritate decesserit: *quod mehercle Christianis nullo modo ferendum est.*" In the same spirit, Jones in his work on the Canon (iii. 252) says, "As we would therefore avoid this consequence of making the authority of this Gospel uncertain, *we must conclude it not to be a translation.*"

Gospel, and there are also strong arguments apparently that St. Matthew wrote his Gospel in Hebrew. So much is this the case, that, as we have seen, many think it best to admit the force of both classes of arguments as irresistible, and simply on this ground, to maintain the hypothesis that the Apostle must have written both in Greek and Hebrew. We shall have occasion afterwards to state our opinion with regard to this mode of evading all difficulties; but in the meantime we confine our remarks to those who take a decided position, either in favour of the Greek or Hebrew original. And in regard to such, we believe that much depends on the *order* in which they are led, either by accident or by their special habits of mind, to consider the complex and conflicting evidence which is available for settling this question. The arguments urged by the defenders of the Hebrew original especially, from their being of such an obvious character, are apt at first to produce a great and, it may be, decided impression. Of this, ample proof is presented in the way in which the subject is sometimes spoken of by writers who have manifestly done little more than glance at the various arguments.[f] And we have ourselves, to some extent, had a personal experience of the effect which is likely in this way to be produced. At first we felt almost compelled, by the force of evidence, to adopt the conclusion that St. Matthew wrote in Hebrew only. Beginning our investigations with a perusal of the arguments of Drs. Davidson and Tregelles, they appeared to us irresistible. It seemed as if the question were finally settled, and that it would be a waste of time longer to

[f] Thus, in an edition of the Gospels, published in 1856, by the Rev. H. C. Adams, late Fellow of Magdalen College, Oxford, we find in the Prolegomena (p. xiii) the following statement with respect to the question, "Whether the Greek version be an original or a translation?"—"When we come to look into the evidence in favour of the latter supposition, we cannot but feel surprised that it should ever have been questioned." We venture to say that the use of such language proves that this writer has hardly done more than, as he expresses it, "look into" the subject. The very fact that such men as Hug *have* questioned, and more than questioned, what he deems so clear, proves that there is more to be said in favour of the Greek original than he has discovered. His words illustrate very plainly the impression which, as stated above, is apt at first to be made by the arguments adduced in support of the Hebrew original.

inquire into the subject. But on further reflection, a very different estimate was formed. We gradually got round to the *opposite point of view*, took a more complete survey of the *whole* evidence, assigned, as it is believed, a juster value to the several parts, and at last reached a firm conviction of the truth, diametrically opposed to that in which for a time we were disposed to acquiesce.

On what principles, then, and in what method *ought* this inquiry to be conducted? These are important questions, the right settlement of which must of necessity have no small influence on the success which will attend our efforts in seeking to reach the truth in this matter; and, before proceeding further, we shall endeavour to give them clear and satisfactory answers. In doing so, it will be seen that, while in some respects we heartily agree with the defenders of the Hebrew original, in others we entirely and essentially differ from them.

Our principles then and method are simply these:—*First*, The question must be decided by *evidence only; Secondly*, We must take into account the *whole evidence;* and *Thirdly*, The *internal* ought, in point of order, to take precedence of the *external* evidence. The validity and import of these three principles will now be illustrated and established.

First, *This question, like all others connected with the Word of God, is to be decided by evidence alone.* In maintaining this proposition, we are quite at one with the upholders of the Hebrew original; but it is necessary, for our own sake, explicitly to state it. Different ground has unfortunately been taken by some with whose conclusions on the general question at issue we agree, however much we may dissent from particular views which they have expressed. There is no principle which we deem more valuable in inquiries of this kind than that of being guided by *evidence only;* and there is no course against which we would more emphatically protest than that of shaping conclusions according to our own preconceived opinions. It is, we hold, utterly improper, and may prove fatally misleading, to allow our own conceptions of what *ought* to be, to have any weight in deciding disputed points in sacred criticism. To attach importance to our own subjective notions, when opposed to evidence, or when unsupported by it, is, in fact, to arrogate to ourselves a position to which we have no rightful claim. For, shall *we* presume to say what God must or ought to have done? Is it for *us* to settle beforehand, either the manner or the contents of any revelation which He may be pleased to make to us? or to dictate the course which, in his Providence, He shall afterwards pursue with regard to it? Surely these are matters which, as every pious and reflecting mind will feel, must be left to His sovereign pleasure; and the only thing which we have to do is to search out and consider the proof with which we are furnished, that He *has* acted in one way or another. Evidence, and not predilection, is the guide which we are bound to follow in every matter connected with Scripture. It *may* happen that, in some instances, a result repugnant to our own wishes will thus be reached. But still, if there is evidence, we must not hesitate. We are bound, if we would act the only part consistent with our character as finite, fallible, and erring creatures, to look to no inward light of our own as the guide to which we will trust—to follow no *ignis fatuus* of our own imagination—but to seek earnestly and diligently for the steady, though often feeble ray of evidence which may come to our aid in the midst of uncertainty, and to surrender ourselves to its guidance exclusively, in our researches after truth.

These statements sound so much like truisms, that there may appear little necessity for making them. But there *is* necessity. Although it might seem that the least reflection on the relative positions of God and man with respect to a divine revelation, the one as supreme, and the other as dependent, would have led to the general adoption and the constant application of the principle which has just been enunciated, this has unhappily not always been the case. A very different spirit has sometimes been manifested by the friends of the Bible. They have either ignored, derided, or defied evidence, in their true but mistaken zeal for the interests of religion; and the consequence has been that they have imperilled that cause which it was their earnest purpose to defend. This is a reproach which, we regret to say, may, with too much justice, be cast upon many of the defenders of the Greek original of St. Matthew's Gospel; and it is a reproach, therefore, from which we must take special care, in entering on this controversy, to stand completely free. But it is not in this question alone that such a spirit has been displayed. It has been exhibited with regard to many other points of sacred criticism; and we gladly take this opportunity of entering our protest against it, whenever and wherever it may be manifested. How often, for example, are Biblical critics assailed with vituperation for simply yielding to the force of evidence. They call in question, it may be, the genuineness of some passages generally received as inspired Scripture, or the validity of some current interpretation, and they are instantly accused of rashness, presumption, or impiety. Now, that not a few critics have justly laid themselves open to these charges, must be admitted. There has been a large class of theologians in Germany, and representatives of whom have not been wanting in this country, who have certainly been guilty of a kind of procedure with respect to the Word of God which is as impious as it is indefensible. They have constituted themselves *arbiters* instead of *inquirers;* they have elevated their own reason to the tribunal of judgment with respect to the *subject-matter* of revelation, instead of humbly employing it as the means of collecting and deciding upon the *evidence* by which that revelation is substantiated, and thus they have presumed to reject as spurious or doubtful whatever did not tally with their own subjective tendencies, and commend itself to their approbation as suitable, necessary, or becoming, in a professed revelation from heaven.

No judgment passed upon such critics can be too severe; but let those who utter it beware lest they themselves incur the same condemnation. It is a curious illustration of the common saying, "extremes meet," to find that the most violent opponents of rationalism have really at times subjected themselves to the very same censure as that which they have so emphatically pronounced. For, what has not unfrequently been their manner of acting? They have, in contravention of all the laws of evidence, clung to certain opinions or prepossessions which have imbedded themselves firmly in their minds; and more than this, they have branded as impious or audacious those who, in a diligent use of their reasoning powers, and a reverent application of the proofs which have been collected, have felt themselves constrained to oppose and condemn certain reigning prejudices and conceptions. Now, in all such cases, we have no hesitation in saying that the charge of presumption is far more applicable to those who advance it, than to those against whom it is directed. For, what is the real meaning of that conduct which, *in spite of evidence*, clings, let us say, to certain passages of the Bible as divine, and which denounces the diligence that discovers, or the honesty that proclaims, their spuriousness? Is it not, in fact, to maintain that the Word of God is *incomplete* without those passages? that they *ought* to have been in it; and that its Author has acted *unwisely*, either in failing to insert them at first, or in allowing them afterwards to be called in question from want of decisive evidence? Such is, in truth, the position assumed by those who persist, on other grounds than those of evidence or rational argument, in maintaining a fixed opinion with respect to any controverted point in sacred criticism; and it needs only to be stated in order to reveal its presumption and impiety. It is in reality to asperse the wisdom of the God both of grace and providence. It is to set the human against the divine: it is to let opinion take the place of fact: it is to elevate subjective feelings to the seat of authority, instead of keeping them, as they ever ought to be kept, thoroughly subordinate to objective truth; and thus, in a word, it is to reach, from a different starting-point, the same conclusion as does the rationalistic interpreter of Scripture. Wherever evidence is, on any pretence, deserted, *there* is the spirit of rationalism displayed. The only legitimate field open to man's researches with respect to revelation is then abandoned; and all the guilt of exalting mere human conceptions, at the expense of divine realities, is unconsciously contracted. The only difference in regard to this matter between the infidel rationalist and the unreasoning dogmatist is, that in the one case there is a bold and reckless avowal made of the standard of judgment which is adopted, and that, in the other, there is an earnest regard professed for the authority of God's Word, while, notwithstanding, the fallible and human is assigned a *sovereign*, and therefore utterly unsuitable and presumptuous place.

Now, it cannot be denied, as has been already said, that those who uphold the Greek original of St. Matthew's Gospel, have sometimes done so on grounds justly liable to the condemnation which has just been expressed. They have allowed their own notions of the probable, or the suitable, to have a very undue influence in deciding the question. This is strikingly observable, for instance, in the writings of Lightfoot. In one place, *e. g.*, he expresses himself as follows: "That which we would have is this,—that Matthew wrote not in Hebrew (he means here *ancient* Hebrew), if so be we suppose him to have written in a language vulgarly known and understood, which certainly we ought to suppose, nor that he nor the other writers of the New Testament writ in the Syriac language, (he means by this *modern* Hebrew, or Aramaic,) unless we suppose them to have written in the *ungrateful* language of an *ungrateful* nation, which certainly *we ought not to suppose.* For, when the Jewish people were now to be cast off, and to be doomed to eternal cursing, it was *very improper certainly* to extol their language, whether it were the Syriac mother-tongue or the Chaldee, its cousin language, into that degree of honour, that it should be the original language of the New Testament. Improper, certainly, it was to write the Gospel in *their* tongue, who above all the inhabitants of the world most despised and opposed it."[g]

Not a few others on the same side, without going to the extreme indicated in these sentences of Lightfoot, have more or less manifested a similar spirit. They have argued, that the inspired original of St. Matthew's Gospel *could* not have been Hebrew, else God would have watched over it, and preserved it from destruction, etc.; or to give the words of Tregelles, when referring to those who have reasoned in this manner: "This dogmatic view of the question has arisen from considerations relative to God, and his mode of acting towards his creatures. It is alleged, that no book which he did not intend for abiding use would be given by inspiration; that no mere translation can be authoritative, and that the old view stamps imperfection on the Canon. It is affirmed, that it is inconceivable that God should not have insured the preservation of an inspired book, and that the contrary would be, in some measure, contradictory to the Divine perfections." Now if, as Dr. Tregelles seems to imply, this mode of arguing has been characteristic of the defenders of the Greek original generally,

[g] Lightfoot's Works, by Pitman, xi. 24.

we beg, for ourselves, most heartily to repudiate it. All such reasonings as those he mentions, appear to us as futile as they are presumptuous. We hold as strongly as he does, that it is no business of ours to inquire what God *would* or *should* have done: we have only to ask what He *has* done. It is not for us to settle *à priori* God's manner of acting in this or in any other doubtful case. We are quite sure that He will always act in a way worthy of Himself, and in harmony with all his infinite perfections; but to attempt to sketch out beforehand how He must therefore have acted in such a matter as the present, appears to us the height of presumption and impiety. For aught we can tell, previous to inquiry, He may have been pleased to give through Matthew, an inspired revelation of his will in Hebrew only, or in Greek only, or in both together: He may have been pleased to let the inspired original perish, and to replace it from the earliest times with an equally inspired translation: or He may have been pleased to allow nothing to come down to us but an imperfect, unauthorized, and misleading version, of what was at first a heaven-inspired and infallible book. One or more of these suppositions may appear to us improbable; but we must not, on that account, refuse to hear the evidence, if any, which can be urged in their support; we dare not say beforehand, which, or how many of them, are certainly true or false; but, in what direction soever our own notions and inclinations may tend, we must set ourselves earnestly and diligently to collect and examine the evidence, and must rest, humbly and willingly, in the conclusion to which that leads. But,—

Secondly, *We must, in examining this question, take into consideration the whole evidence.* This is a statement which bears as much the appearance of a truism as the former, but which has also, we believe, been to a great extent overlooked in dealing with this question. The principle which it contains is not less important than that which has already been considered, for it is manifest that a false result is as likely to be reached by taking a *one-sided* view of the evidence, as by ignoring it altogether. And in this, we believe, is to be found the *causa erroris* in the case of those who have pronounced so decisively in favour of the Hebrew original. They have looked only at *one* department of the evidence, and have, in fact, not unfrequently argued as if that were the whole. Take, *e. g.*, one of the ablest advocates of this hypothesis, Dr. Tregelles, and let us observe the manner in which he discusses the question. His first sentence is sufficient to set his method before us. "In the following remarks," he says,[h] "I propose to consider what was the original language in which St. Matthew wrote his Gospel, by an examination of ancient evidence in connexion with the circumstances which relate to that testimony." By this "ancient evidence," as soon appears, he means only the *statements* made upon the subject by ancient writers; and nothing else is taken into account by him in settling the point at issue. But is it not manifest, that in a question such as the present, there are other things that ought to be considered, than simply what may have been *said* upon the subject? This would be the case, even although no Greek Gospel were extant at the present day. If no book at all now existed, bearing the name of St. Matthew, we should still be warranted in subjecting the statements of antiquity, as to the language in which that Apostle once wrote, to the test of other ascertained circumstances. Every one acquainted with history, knows how many assertions made by ancient writers require to be set aside, because proved inconsistent with other known facts. And it would be to claim infallibility for those ancient fathers who have left us a statement of their opinions on this subject, did we not venture to inquire, by the aid of other existing facts or probabilities, whether they may not possibly have been mistaken. If, then, I repeat, we had no Gospel at all bearing the name, and ascribed to the authorship of the Apostle Matthew, at the present day, we should still be justified, (and required, if the question were of any importance,) in considering the statements made regarding his work by ancient writers, in the light of facts which had been ascertained as to the state of things in which they wrote, their sources of information, the consistency and independence of their testimony, etc., and thus deciding as to the probability or improbability of their assertions.

But the case is much stronger, when we actually hold in our

[h] I refer here, and throughout this treatise, to Tregelles "On the Original Language of St. Matthew's Gospel." (Bagsters, 1850.) The same dissertation had previously appeared in "The Journal of Sacred Literature." First Series, vol. v.

hands a Gospel in Greek, bearing the name of the Apostle, and transmitted to us from the earliest times as an integral portion of the New Testament Scriptures. The question as to its original language, cannot in such a case be settled by the mere citation of passages from writers in the second, third, or fourth centuries. The *Gospel itself*, in its present form, runs up into a higher antiquity, as is generally admitted, than belongs to any of those testimonies which attribute to it a different original language from that in which we now possess it. It existed, as most allow, in *Greek*, before the Apostles left the earth; it exists in that language still; and surely, therefore, it ought *itself* to be taken into account, as forming an essential part of the evidence in that question which we are called upon to consider.

Moreover, there are other indisputable facts connected with the volume of which the Greek Gospel of St. Matthew forms a part, which have a manifest bearing upon the discussion, and must not be overlooked. How is it possible, *e. g.*, with any propriety, to leave out of view in dealing with this question, the striking and important fact, that our present Gospel of St. Matthew abounds in *verbal coincidences* with the other Gospels, all of which are now universally admitted to have been written in the Greek language? There *may be* a satisfactory mode of explaining this fact, without adopting our supposition, that St. Matthew's Gospel, like the rest, was written in Greek—a point to be afterwards fully considered—but at any rate, the striking phenomenon which has been mentioned, cannot properly be overlooked in discussing this question. Yet overlooked it *has* been by most of the defenders of the Hebrew original. In their excessive zeal for "ancient evidence," they have forgotten what is both the most ancient and the most trustworthy of all—the phenomena presented by the Gospel itself. St. Matthew has a voice, as well as St. Jerome, in the settlement of this question. But that voice has been almost entirely disregarded by the defenders of the Hebrew original. They have eagerly inquired what Papias and Origen had to say in the matter; but they scarcely think it worth their trouble to ask of the writer of the Gospel himself, what testimony *he* bears, *by the special character attaching to his work*, as to the language in which it was originally given to the world.

We complain, then, with regard to the upholders of the Hebrew original, that they do not take into account the *whole* evidence. Dr. Tregelles very frequently, and very warmly contends for the paramount authority of *evidence* in settling this and all other Biblical questions; and in this, as has been already seen, we most cordially agree with him. But, then, he appears to us most unduly to *limit* the evidence. It is only one kind of proof at which he will look; and that, as we believe, by no means the surest or strongest kind—the proof which is furnished in the express declarations of ancient writers. And it is on these, almost exclusively, that the assailants of the true originality of our Greek Gospel rest their cause. Quotations from the ancient fathers are marshalled so thick and deep, that *these* are seen, and scarcely anything besides. Indeed, as was previously hinted, it is no easy matter for an unprejudiced inquirer ever to get round to the other side of the question at all. As soon as he enters on the investigation, his judgment is apt to be greatly biassed, if, indeed, it is not completely decided, by the arguments thus prominently presented by the writers referred to; and he certainly has no chance of hearing from them the caution, that a *full half at least* of the evidence remains yet to be considered. The consequence is, that he may scarcely look at the remaining evidence at all, but may rest in the conclusion already formed: whereas, had he followed out the inquiry by contemplating the question from a different stand-point, he might have been led to a very different result. We are greatly disposed to believe, from what almost happened to ourselves, that not a few who look into this controversy, never succeed in obtaining more than a *partial* view of the various considerations which make up our available data for determining this question. Their opinion is formed in favour of the Hebrew original, while one important branch of the evidence remains wholly unconsidered. And if they are persuaded to devote attention to that at all, it is only to deny that it should have any great influence in the controversy, and to explain away all that seems inconsistent with the conclusion which has been already reached.

We repeat, therefore, our second principle,—that the *whole* evidence must be considered. Quotations from ancient writers, statements by early fathers, are only one element in deciding this question. The entire mass of evidence, internal as well as external, must be taken into account, and the judgment must be guided by a fair and candid estimation of the whole. In all questions, of course, except those capable of mathematical certainty, the arguments brought forward will be more or less conflicting, sometimes being so equally balanced as to leave the problem utterly insolvable, and sometimes so largely on one side as almost to amount to demonstration. But in the most difficult and perplexing cases, we have *this* rule to guide us,—that the same principle which renders it our duty to follow evidence at all, also requires that we should submit to the *preponderating* evidence, although unable satisfactorily to explain that which points to a different conclusion. This may be our position with respect to the present question. We may find enough of evidence on the one side to convince us that *there* lies the truth, and yet may not be able completely to meet every objection which may be urged on the other. If the proof on one side is of *such a nature* as is irresistible, then the most which can be demanded is, that we furnish a possible or plausible explanation of the difficulties felt on the other. If again, the argument does not seem wholly conclusive on either side, our duty will be discharged by taking a full and impartial view of the entire evidence attainable, and then, by forming our judgment according to probability, which, as Butler remarks, is to us "the very guide of life."

But now the question occurs,—In what *order* is the evidence to be adduced? What arguments are to be first considered? This, as has been said, is an important point in such an inquiry as the present; and with regard to it we observe,—

Thirdly, *That the logical and natural course is to allow the internal to take precedence of the external evidence.* In maintaining this proposition, it seems almost sufficient to state, that there are circumstances easily conceivable in a work such as St. Matthew's Gospel, *which render it perfectly impossible that it can be a translation.* The existence of such circumstances, or not, can only be ascertained by an actual inspection of the document; and therefore, the proper course manifestly is, first to examine the history itself, before allowing our judgment to be swayed by the statements which have been made respecting it.

It is scarcely needful to illustrate the assertion which has just been made, that a writing *may* possess in itself sure and evident marks that it is, or is not, a translation. This is the case with most versions, and most originals, in every language. In spite of what has been said to the contrary, we hold that there is, after all, nothing which is more certainly within the power of literary tact and experience, than in all ordinary cases, to distinguish between an original and a translated work. No two languages approach so closely to each other in idiom, as to allow a translator, who is scrupulously faithful to the work he has undertaken, an opportunity of imparting to his production the air and character of an original. In cases of very free translation, such as Pope's translation of Homer, the traces of the original language may be almost, or altogether obliterated.; but this cannot take place, when (as is claimed for our Greek Gospel of St. Matthew) a close and faithful adherence is preserved to the original. A foreign and awkward air will almost inevitably attach to every translation from one language into another, if any approach to *literal exactness* is sought to be maintained in the version that is produced. It is sufficient to refer in proof of this, to the Septuagint translation from the Hebrew into Greek, to the many close translations from the German or French into our own language at the present day, or to the versions of the ancient classics into the various tongues of modern Europe. In all such cases, a person of ordinary ability and experience would have no difficulty in at once detecting the translation, and in assigning the reasons which had led him to that conclusion.

Dr. Tregelles, however, seems inclined to deny this; and asks what traces the Lord's Prayer in English bears of being a translation. We may admit that no such traces are to be found, without any prejudice to our argument. The unfairness of comparing *a few lines*, with the Gospel of St. Matthew *at large*, must be apparent to every reader. The Lord's Prayer is so short as to form no parallel to an extensive work like the entire evangelical history; and no one, we suppose, will deny, that *detached passages* may easily be found in any translation which will pass as original. And besides, the Lord's Prayer is a composition of such a nature, that the points which specially mark a translation, are necessarily wanting in it. It consists of a number of independent clauses, each complete in itself, so that the different modes of connecting one part of a sentence with another, which serve specially to distinguish different languages, cannot appear. Indeed, *one* of its petitions might as fairly be made the test of its being a translation, as the *whole*.

But whether it be possible or not to detect a translation by its intrinsic character, it is certain, at all events, that a work may contain in itself, plain and unmistakeable proof that it is *an original and not a translation*. How certain is it, *e. g.*, that the history of Thucydides, the odes of Horace, and the dramas of Shakspeare, are original, and not translated works! They bear evidence, not only in the style and idiom in which they are written, but by the manner in which they reflect the life and habits of the age and country in which they were respectively composed, as well as by the frequent allusions which they contain to national affairs and contemporary occurrences, that they were written originally by the persons whose names they bear, and could not possibly have been translations made by them, or any others, from a different language. Not the most united external testimony would ever persuade the world to the contrary, or lessen, in the faintest degree, the conviction arising from a perusal of the works themselves, that they were written originally in the language in which we still possess them.

Since, then, it is quite possible that internal evidence *may* exist, which renders it absolutely certain that our present Greek Gospel of St. Matthew is not a translation, but an original work, it is plainly the proper and logical course, first of all, to inquire whether or not such is to be found. If we adopt the opposite course, and begin first with a consideration of the evidence of testimony, then, after reaching our conclusion with respect to it, we may find, on turning to the Gospel itself, that that conclusion cannot be sustained, as being inconsistent with other plain and incontrovertible facts. When any one, therefore, tells us, on our taking the existing Gospel of St. Matthew into our hands—as the advocates of its Hebrew origin do tell us—that it is a translation, and not an original work, the first and most obvious question to be considered is the evidence borne by the Gospel itself with respect to that assertion. On opening and examining it, we may find proof the most conclusive either for or against such a declaration. It may appear either plain, probable, possible, or impossible, that our present Gospel is a translation. There are works, as every one knows, which are seen on the very first look to be translations; and there are also other works, as has been said, of which it may most confidently be maintained, on an examination of their contents, that they are originals. Others still, let us admit, may be found, of which it cannot be positively declared on internal grounds, whether they are originals or translations, but which may be accepted as either, according to the external evidence which accompanies them. If it is found, on an inspection of our Gospel, that it bears plain or probable evidence of being a translation, then the statements which have been made to that effect may at once be received; if, on the other hand, it clearly appears that it cannot be a translation, then the statements in question must be resolved into a misapprehension; and if finally, it is difficult or impossible to say, from internal considerations, whether it be a translation or an original work, then the preponderating external evidence may be allowed to decide the question.

Such, then, is the course of argument to be followed in the present discussion. We are to look first at the internal evidence, and allow it to determine the weight which is to be assigned to the external. This we hold to be the logical and natural method; and it is a method, we trust, which commends itself to the approbation of our readers. We can scarcely hope, indeed, that writers like Dr. Tregelles, who is in the habit of almost ignoring *internal* evidence on all critical subjects, will not object to the course which has been indicated. To such an extent does the eminent critic referred to carry his repugnance to all objective proof of an intrinsic character, that he seems in one passage to deny it the very name of evidence, and that, although it may amount to demonstration. He says, "It has been argued that our Greek Gospel *must* be an original document. If this must be the case, let it once be demonstrated, and then *evidence* may be overlooked." Here there seems to be furnished a striking proof of that one-sidedness, which, as was before shown, has greatly characterized the defenders of the Hebrew original. Dr. Tregelles appears to imagine that there is nothing which can be called evidence on the other side at all. And yet, with curious inconsistency, he calls for a *demonstration* from that side, and "then," he adds, "evidence may be overlooked!" Why, how could the supposed demonstration be effected except by evidence? and how could evidence be overlooked after that demonstration had been accomplished? There remains, in fact, *no evidence to be overlooked*, when demonstration has been reached: all the counter statements which may then be made, can only be regarded as a congeries of errors.

But, although we can hardly hope for the concurrence of Dr. Tregelles in the justness and propriety of that methed which has been indicated, we are not without the sanction of some other eminent critics. Thus Credner,[1] after bringing forward very fully the testimonies usually quoted from the fathers, to the effect that St. Matthew wrote his Gospel in Hebrew, still holds that the question, whether or not our present Greek Gospel is a translation, remains undecided, and that it can only be settled by a consideration of its internal character. "What Biblical criticism, then," he says, "has to do in this matter, is simply to concern itself with the following question,—whether or not our present Gospel of St. Matthew bears evidence in itself that it is a translation from the Hebrew."

And it is curious to observe, that even Eichhorn, one of the

[1] Einleitung in das N. T. § 46. Credner is here labouring to reach the conclusion that our existing Gospel is not Apostolic; but we may quote his authority as to the *method* in which the question, *whether or not it is a translation*, should be settled, while far from agreeing in the opinion which he adopts as to its canonical authority. And we may take this opportunity of observing, that however much one may regret the rationalistic tendencies of Credner, it is impossible not to admire the clearness and fulness with which he treats of every point which falls under his consideration. As Moses Stuart remarks (Fosdick's Hug, p. 703) regarding an expected publication of Credner, "This must be a work full of interest, when in such hands as those of Credner, and this will be true whether the *theory* he adopts be right or wrong; for in whatever direction he moves, he never makes an idle or insignificant movement." I willingly confess myself more indebted to Credner for full and available information on the points touched upon in this treatise, than to any other critic.

most determined upholders of the Hebrew original, also expresses himself, as if he deemed the proof of translation incomplete without taking into consideration our existing Greek Gospel. He proceeds, from a consideration of the passages usually quoted from the ancients in this controversy, to an examination of the arguments which he imagines may be derived from the Gospel itself in support of this hypothesis, and heads the chapter in which he treats of these, "*Decisive* proof that St. Matthew wrote in Hebrew," etc.[k]

Since, then, one critic (Credner) believes that the Gospel itself bears in its structure plain marks of its originality, and another (Eichhorn) supposes that it furnishes in the same way decisive proof of its being a translation, the *internal* evidence is thus acknowledged on both sides as being the dominating element in the settlement of this question, and naturally therefore, in the first place, demands our attention.

Before, however, proceeding to an examination of the Gospel itself, there is a preliminary inquiry which has been felt by all writers on this subject to deserve some attention. We refer to the question which has been agitated respecting the language that prevailed in Palestine in the days of Christ and his Apostles. Different views have been taken of this point by the supporters of the Greek and Hebrew original of St. Matthew's Gospel respectively. Sometimes, indeed, they approach very nearly to each other. Not a few of the advocates of the Hebrew original candidly admit the wide extent to which the Greek language then prevailed in Palestine. Others, however, with more regard to the safety of their argument, are inclined to restrict the extent, in which it was understood and employed, within the narrowest limits. And the reason why they should endeavour to do so is evident. Their whole argument rests on the assumption, that Hebrew was then the language which a Jew would naturally and most fittingly employ in addressing his Jewish countrymen. "We are far from denying,"[1] says Dr. Davidson, "that the Greek language prevailed to a great extent in Palestine in the age

[k] Einleitung in das N. T. i. 106. "Entscheidender Beweis für einem hebräischen Grundtext: Fehler des griechischen Uebersetzers."

[1] Introduction to the New Test. vol. i. 41.

of Christ and his apostles. But there is abundant evidence to show that the Aramæan prevailed at the same time, and we believe, to a greater extent: that it was the national language to which the Jews were accustomed from their earliest years, and which they naturally liked the best. When, therefore, it is considered that Matthew as a Jew wrote a Gospel for the use of his Jewish brethren in Palestine, it is reasonable to conclude that he would employ the language for which they had a predilection."

In the opinion here expressed, that Matthew wrote specially for the Jews, we willingly concur. We say *specially*, not *exclusively*, as seems to be for the most part taken for granted by the defenders of the Hebrew original. If there are in our first Gospel, indications that it was in some degree particularly designed for the Jewish converts in Palestine, there are also, we believe, at least as convincing proofs contained in it, that it was intended for universal circulation. This appears, not only from such explanations as occur in it (i. 23; xxvii. 8, 33, 46),—which, being totally useless to Jewish readers, are supposed by Dr. Davidson and others to have been inserted by the Greek translator,—but from passages which have a universal reference (xxvi. 13; xxviii. 19), and which must have formed part of the Gospel from the very first.

Bearing in mind, then, that we maintain the universal no less than the special design of St. Matthew's Gospel, (just as we hold that St. Luke wrote for all the world, though, in the first instance, he addressed himself to Theophilus,) let the following additional sentences from Dr. Davidson be considered:—" The prevalence of the Greek language," he says,[m] " in Palestine, has been largely insisted on by Hug, and others, as an argument for the Greek original. But when it is remembered that this Gospel was written for the Jews in Palestine,—a fact expressly attested by ancient writers, and confirmed by its internal character,—it will be found that the currency of Greek in Judæa is not decisive of the question. If it could be shown that the Greek had *entirely supplanted* Syro-Chaldaic, or that the Jews at least *preferred* it, then, indeed, it might be concluded, that a Greek Gospel alone

[m] Introduction, i. 37.

was written by Matthew for the use of his countrymen; but as long as neither prevailed exclusively in the land, there is room for hesitation in arriving at that conclusion."

This extract is worthy of notice in several respects. It shows how important is the question respecting the reigning language of Palestine at the time, to the upholders of the Hebrew original. Sometimes it has been said, that the hypothesis of the Greek original rests on the opinion that Greek was the prevailing language of Judæa in the days of Christ; but it may with far greater truth be maintained, that the hypothesis of the Hebrew original has nothing else on which to rest, than the assumption that Hebrew was then the ordinary language of the country. It is very easy to see that important purposes might be served by the Apostle writing in Greek, even although that language was not the prevailing language of Palestine. He thus made himself intelligible to the world at large, while at the same time he certainly was not unintelligible even to the natives of Judæa. The expediency of an early authoritative history of the life of Christ, being published in a language which all could understand, must be universally admitted;[n] and this *was* effected by the preparation of St Matthew's Gospel, provided he wrote in Greek and not in Hebrew.

But, on the other hand, no reason whatever can be assigned for his having written in Hebrew, unless it can be proved that that was the only, or the common language then made use of in Palestine. Every one admits that he could never have written his Gospel in Aramaic with a view to its universal diffusion, since that language was never understood beyond a very limited territory. And very strong cause, certainly, ought to be shown, why the first inspired account of a religion destined for all nations, should have been written in a tongue known to one nation only, and that, while another language existed, which it is admitted was in no small degree familiar to that nation, and was at the same time generally known throughout the world.

Another observation may be made on the words of Dr. Davidson,

[n] See this point illustrated in Townson's "Discourses on the Gospels," vol. i. 83.

quoted above. He admits, that if it can be shown that the Jews "preferred" Greek in addressing each other, the question is to be regarded as settled in favour of the Greek original. We accept the challenge. We undertake to prove, by an induction of facts, that the Jews of that time *did prefer* Greek as the language of religious address. If we succeed in this, then, in the estimation of one of the most strenuous defenders of the Hebrew original, that opinion must be abandoned. We shall hear no more of the statements of antiquity. Papias and all his followers will be acknowledged in error. The whole cause of the Hebrew original, as is thus confessed, stands or falls according to the manner in which this question regarding the language of Palestine in the days of Christ is settled; and the investigation of this subject has therefore a very essential bearing on our argument.

The inquiry, however, respecting the language commonly made use of in Palestine at the commencement of our era, and which was, therefore, for the most part employed by Christ, is highly interesting and important, on other grounds than that connected with the language of St. Matthew's Gospel. It is a question, we believe, on the right settlement of which depends the solution of some other very difficult and perplexing questions connected with our existing Gospels. On the ground, therefore, of its general importance, no less than of its vital influence on the special subject of inquiry pursued in this treatise, we shall, in the following chapter enter at some length into the argument, and set before our readers the grounds of that conclusion, which we deem its only true and satisfactory settlement.

# CHAPTER II.

## LANGUAGE OF PALESTINE IN THE DAYS OF CHRIST AND HIS APOSTLES.

### SECTION I.—GENERAL OBSERVATIONS.

THE object of this Chapter is to prove, chiefly from the New Testament itself, that Greek was widely diffused, well understood, and commonly employed in Palestine in the time of Christ and his Apostles.

In maintaining this proposition, we do not mean to deny that the Hebrew language, in the form of Aramæan, also existed throughout the country, and was, to a considerable extent, made use of among the people. The real state of matters, we believe, to have been this: that almost all the Jews, *in* Palestine as well as *out* of it, were then, as Salmasius expresses it, "bilingues;" that is, they understood both the Greek, the common language, and their own vernacular dialect, the proper tongue of the region in which they lived. In this view of the case, the two languages made use of by the Jews of Palestine would be the Hebrew (in its modernized and corrupted form[o])—their true ancestral dialect, and the Greek, which had, through force of circumstances, been introduced into their country, and flourished side by side with their mother-tongue. The condition of the Palestinian Jews at the date referred to, thus appears to us to have been very similar to that of some of our English colonies at the present day. In several of these we find two different languages simultaneously existing, one of which is the language of the conquerors, and the

[o] To prevent misconception, it may be well to state here, once for all, that by *Hebrew* is meant throughout this treatise the Aramæan or Syro-Chaldaic language, except where it is plainly stated that the *ancient* Hebrew is intended.

other of which is a form, more or less corrupted, of the ancient vernacular language of the country. "In Canada," for example, as Latham writes, "the English language first took root after the taking of Quebec, in the reign of George the Second. As Canada, however, had been previously a French colony, the European language that was first spoken there was not the English, but the French. Hence, when Quebec was taken, the language of the country fell into two divisions. There were the different dialects of the original Indians, and there was the French of the first European colonists. At the present moment, both these languages maintain their ground; so that the English is spoken only partially in Canada, the French and the Indian existing by the side of it.

"At the Cape of Good Hope, the English is spoken in a similar manner; that is, it is spoken partially. The original inhabitants were the Caffre and Hottentot tribes of Africa, and the earliest European colonists were the Dutch. For these reasons, Dutch and English, conjointly with the Hottentot and Caffrarian dialects, form the languages of the Cape of Good Hope. In Guiana, too, in South America, English and Dutch are spoken in the neighbourhood of each other, for the same reason as at the Cape."[p]

Or, as perhaps still more accurately and clearly representing the state of things which we conceive to have then existed in Palestine, we may briefly refer to the linguistic peculiarity observable at the present day in the islands of the English Channel. In these islands—Guernsey, for instance—almost all the inhabitants understand and employ English; but, side by side with that language, there exists a kind of impure French, which is largely made use of by the lower orders of the people. An Englishman, mixing only among the educated classes on the island, would never suspect that any other language than his own was in common use among its population; but if he penetrate a mile or two into the interior, and accost any of the peasantry in their homes or at their labours, he will soon hear the tones of a foreign tongue, and will find that *it* is generally preferred, in the rural districts, to the language of England. Hence it comes to pass that both

[p] Latham on the English Language, vol. i. 376.

English and French—each language, in many instances, more or less influenced by the other—are known by almost all the natives of the island; and while the educated classes generally make use of the former, the lower orders as generally prefer the latter.

Now this very nearly represents what we conceive to have been the state of matters in Palestine in the days of Christ. The Greek, we believe, to have been almost universally prevalent, and to have been understood and employed, more or less, by all classes in the community; but to have been attended by the Aramæan, which was spoken partially and occasionally by all ranks of the native population, being among such the language of homely and familiar intercourse, and still, though with difficulty, maintaining its position as the vernacular language of the country.

It will be observed, then, that we put in no claim for the Greek as having been the *only* language in common use among the Jews in the days of Christ. We simply maintain that it was the *prevailing* language,—the language especially of literature and commerce; the language which a religious teacher would have no hesitation in selecting and making use of, *for the most part*, as the vehicle of conveying his instructions, whether orally or in writing, and which was, accordingly, thus employed both by our Saviour and his Apostles.

Some have taken much higher, and others greatly lower ground on this subject. About a century ago, a treatise was published at Naples by Diodati, in which the learned and ingenious author labours to prove that Greek had, in the days of our Lord, entirely supplanted the old Palestinian dialect, and was in fact the only language then generally known among the people. In this particular object, we think it must be admitted that the author fails; but he collects much and varied information bearing upon the general question, and his argument, though pressed somewhat too far, is, we believe, in the main points established, and is conducted throughout with a lucidity of statement and a liveliness of style which render it extremely interesting and attractive.[q]

[q] The title of this excellent little treatise is as follows:—"Dominici Diodati J. C. Neapolitani, de Christo Græce loquente." 8vo, Neapoli, 1767. It had become so rare that Hug states he could not procure a copy of it, even at Naples; but it is now accessible to all scholars in a neat and convenient form,

On the other side it has been maintained, that the Greek language was scarcely used at all in ordinary intercourse by the Jews of our Saviour's day; and that, accordingly, Aramaic was the language which He generally or exclusively employed. Among the supporters of this view, Dr. Pfannkuche may perhaps be referred to as chief. This writer had never himself seen the work of Diodati; but his treatise may, nevertheless, be regarded as a formal reply to that of the Neapolitan scholar, inasmuch as he made use of the previous reply of De Rossi, which had been published at Parma in 1772. Respecting De Rossi, Hug observes, that he "sometimes confounds different periods, often uses poor weapons, but is a stout combatant;" and in all these respects he found in Dr. Pfannkuche a not unworthy successor. There is, as every reader must feel, a most irritating want of method, clearness, and logical coherence in the work of the learned German; in these particulars, no less than in its special object, his treatise is the very antithesis of Diodati's; and were the question in debate to be settled by an appeal to the literary ability displayed by the respective champions, there could be little doubt in whose favour judgment would instantly be pronounced.[r]

We deem it needless, in proceeding to support our position on this question, to enter very minutely into the external or historical part of the argument, since that ground has already been well traversed by some previous writers. In addition to Diodati, the learned Professor Hug in particular has laboured very assiduously in this department of the evidence, and has accumulated much valuable information on the point at issue. But both Diodati and Hug, as well as all the other writers on this question with whom we are acquainted, have left one important branch of the

having been republished in this country, some years ago, by Dr. Dobbin, of Trinity College, Dublin. Diodati was a civilian, and not an ecclesiastic, as he is sometimes naturally but erroneously called.

[r] The work of Pfannkuche was translated and published in this country in Vol. II. of the Cabinet Library. We shall have occasion in the sequel to advert to some of the halting conclusions of this writer: meanwhile, in illustration of what is said above, we may simply refer to page 15 of the translation, where we find the translator *naively* remarking on a statement in the original—"It was not well done in Dr. Pf. to keep for himself the *more decisive* proofs!"

argument almost entirely untouched. They are very painstaking and successful in collecting historical proofs from other ancient writings and monuments as to the prevalence of Greek in Palestine at the commencement of our era; but their references to the evidence of this fact, which is contained in the books of the New Testament itself, are meagre and insufficient. And yet it is manifest that, on the supposition of the several parts of the New Testament being the genuine products of the age in which they profess to have been written, they must yield us no small assistance in dealing with this question. They form indeed by far the largest and most reliable portion of that evidence which we possess upon the subject. This would at once have been perceived and acted upon had these books happened to be the productions of secular instead of sacred writers. If we possessed such a number of the works of other Jews who lived in that age, as we have in the New Testament, which contains histories and epistles by no fewer than eight different Jewish authors, most of them natives of Palestine, it would have been felt that little difficulty ought to remain as to the language which then prevailed among them. But it has happened here as with some other more important points connected with our religion. That tendency which has led in many cases to the neglect of the strong confirmation of the truth of Christianity which is to be found in the acceptance of it as divine, by such a man as Paul, *simply because he did accept it*, has also led to the overlooking of the evidence which the New Testament itself furnishes as to the language of Palestine in the age in which it was written, *simply because it is the New Testament*. To this comparatively neglected portion of the evidence, then, we propose principally to direct attention; and before proceeding to do so, we shall merely give an outline of what may, by way of distinction, be called the historical argument, and state the leading facts, which, as we believe, have in this department been conclusively established.

## SECTION II.—HISTORICAL PROOFS OF THE PREVALENCE OF GREEK IN PALESTINE IN THE DAYS OF CHRIST AND HIS APOSTLES.

It must be admitted by all that the Greek tongue had become very widely and generally known throughout the world before the birth of Christ. Greek, indeed, was then the common language of all civilized nations,[a] and thus formed a medium of intercourse between countries far separated in geographical position, as well as differing greatly in national habits and institutions. Many and powerful causes had contributed to this result. A foundation was laid for it in the transcendant merits of the language itself. Never has a tongue been spoken by man which can vie with the Greek in all that constitutes the excellency of a language. In copiousness, plasticity, melody, and power, it has ever been, and probably will ever remain, unrivalled. It was natural, therefore, that as the world advanced, under the wise and benignant providence of God, in knowledge and civilization, this pre-eminent language should more and more attract attention and acquire ascendancy. It was in itself the very queen of languages, and it could not but happen that, as refinement and the desire for intellectual improvement advanced throughout the earth, its manifest title to supremacy, as the best means ever devised for expressing all kinds of human thought, should be more and more practically acknowledged and proved.

And, as contributing to this result, there must also be taken into account the literary treasures which, from a very early date in the history of nations, it had contained. Not only was the Greek language in itself an instrument of exceeding beauty and power, but that instrument had been so employed as to give rise to many of the very master-pieces of human intellect and genius. In poetry, in philosophy, in history, and in eloquence, Greece had already, centuries before the Christian era, poured forth, in her own unequalled tongue, effusions of still unequalled excellence;—

[a] "Die griechische Sprache war damals in der ganzen gesitteten Welt verbreitet."—De Wette, Einleitung in das N. T. § 1.

so perfect, indeed, that it has been the highest ambition, and well nigh the despair, of all subsequent ages, simply to imitate and approach them. It was doubly impossible, therefore, if the world continued in a course of progressive improvement, that the tongue of Greece should not be more and more studied and prevail. Mankind, advancing in knowledge and refinement, could not remain satisfied without a wide-spread acquaintance with the language of Homer, Plato, and Demosthenes; and however much the political influence of Greece might wane among the nations, it was certain that, if light and literature continued to spread, her intellectual dominion would survive and increase. The familiar line of Horace in which he tells us of his own country, that "Græcia capta ferum victorem cepit," just expresses what must in every case have happened unless mankind were to retrograde instead of advancing,—to relapse into barbarism and darkness, instead of pressing forward in the path of intelligence and improvement.

But besides these resistless intrinsic claims on the homage and submission of mankind, there were other events of an external character that powerfully tended to the dissemination and supremacy of the Greek literature and language. The triumphant march of the great Alexander from his native Macedon to the banks of the Indus, the complete subjugation of so many different nations by his arms, the settlement of Greek princes on the thrones of those mighty kingdoms into which, on his death, his colossal empire was divided, and the establishment of numerous colonies of Greeks throughout the countries which he had subdued, necessarily led to the very wide diffusion of the Greek language, and to a general tendency to imitate Greek manners and institutions. And, as was to be expected from the combined operation of all these causes, we have the amplest and clearest testimony to the wide-spread ascendancy which had been gained by the tongue of Greece before the birth of Christ. A familiar acquaintance with it was more or less possessed by almost all those nations which were then embraced under the sway of imperial Rome. The language had, of course, become greatly corrupted. Ionic softness and Attic elegance had in many instances been replaced by a worse than Doric or Æolian harshness. But still the language of Herodotus and Euripides had in its substance pervaded the Roman dominions, and was in reality the link by which the most distant portions of the world owning Cæsar's rule were socially and intellectually held together.[t] In the gigantic[u] capital itself, which might have been regarded as the empire in miniature, since under its ample wings were gathered representatives from the farthest provinces, the Greek tongue was continually employed. In the reign of Tiberius, as Valerius Maximus, a contemporary writer, informs us, the senate resounded even to deafening with *Greek* debates;[v] and in this, as well as many similar intimations contained in the classical writers, we find proof that, while almost countless dialects might have been heard among the vast and multifarious population of Rome, the various tribes there mixed together possessed in the language of ancient Greece, then become the language of the world, a means whereby they could communicate with one another.

Greek, then, and not Latin, was really the language of the Roman empire. As Cicero himself tells us (Pro Arch. Poet. § 23), "Græca leguntur in omnibus fere gentibus, Latina suis finibus, exiguis sane, continentur." And, as being in striking harmony with this statement, such facts as the following might in no small number be adduced. The Apostle Paul, as all acknowledge, wrote *to* the Romans in Greek: Clement of Rome wrote *from* that city in Greek: Ignatius, like Paul, addressed the Roman churches in Greek; and Irenæus wrote from Lyons in Greek on a theme interesting to, and intended to be considered by, the whole Christian world.

[t] "Die griechische Sprache damals in der ganzen gesitteten Welt verbreitet war, und man mit ihr in ganzen Umfange des Romischen Reichs sich verständlich machen konnte."—Guerike, Neut. Isagog. § 10.

[u] Truly gigantic, if the calculations of some recent writers are to be trusted. De Quincey, in the last published volume of his works (January, 1859), describes the Rome of the Cæsars as "a city which counted from one horn to the other of its mighty suburbs not less than *four millions* of inhabitants at the very least, as we resolutely maintain after reviewing all that has been written on that much vexed theme, and not impossibly half as many more." This immense assemblage of human beings, collected from almost every nation under heaven, must have had a common language, and that could be no other than the Greek.

[v] Val. Max. ii. 2, 3, quoted by Hug, ii. 10.

There seems to have existed among the Romans, during the period to which we refer, a strong and universal passion for the Greek language and literature. Hence we find Cicero often complaining, with no small bitterness, of the neglect with which writings in the proper language of Latium were received;[w] and hence also we learn, without surprise, that Greek was employed in all parts of the empire by Roman orators, generals, and magistrates. Cicero himself spoke in Greek in the senate at Syracuse. Crassus, when as proconsul he made war against Aristonicus in Asia, shewed himself so familiar with the Greek language, that he even addressed each of the Greek tribes in its own proper dialect, speaking to the Ionians in Ionic, and to the Æolians in Æolic. Augustus, as conqueror and sovereign, addressed the people of Alexandria in Greek; and Mucian, as Tacitus informs us (Hist. ii. 80), induced the inhabitants of Antioch, by his persuasive eloquence in the Greek language (Græcâ facundiâ), to espouse the cause of Vespasian.

These facts, with many others of a similar nature which meet us in the literature of the period, are more than enough to prove the general, we might almost say universal, use which was made of the Greek language throughout the Roman empire. And now the question arises, *Is there any reason to suppose that Palestine formed an exception?* Must we believe that while Greek was so prevalent, as has been seen, in other parts of the Roman world, there were special causes at work which prevented its introduction into Judæa, or which kept it from being generally known and employed in that country? Unless this can be shown, the evidence already brought forward to prove that Greek prevailed generally throughout the Roman empire, must be held also to prove that it prevailed in Palestine, and that, just as St. Paul naturally wrote to the Romans in Greek, so St. Matthew *most probably* addressed the Jews in the same language.

Now we *do* find that there were for several generations before Christ special causes at work among the Jews of Palestine, which were certain to have a great effect upon the language of that country. But these causes *favoured*, instead of impeding a gene-

[w] See, *e.g.*, his treatise "De Finibus," lib. i. 1, 2, 3, etc.

ral acquaintance with Greek among the people. This has been largely shown by Diodati in the first part of his treatise, and is also very clearly brought out by Hug in his discussion of the question at issue. But we do not propose, as has been said, to enter at length into this division of the argument. We hasten on to other and less trodden ground. And, therefore, referring to the writers mentioned for full details, we shall here content ourselves with simply quoting the masterly summary, presented by Credner, of the various causes which had for long been operating in Palestine, and which, by their united influence, had brought about a general acquaintance with Greek among its population.

"Ever since the times of Alexander the Great, the Jews had emigrated in great numbers from Palestine to Greek countries. In these lands, even the more educated among them, such as Philo, forgot their mother-tongue: and this happened all the more readily, since, from their sacred books having been translated into the Greek language, provision had thus been made even for their religious necessities. At the same time, these Grecian Jews, known as Hellenists, remained in unbroken communion with their native country. Jerusalem was always regarded by the Jews as their capital: the Sanhedrim of that city was in all religious points their highest authority; and thousands of Greek-speaking Jews travelled annually to Palestine, in order that, in the national sanctuary at Jerusalem, they might present their supplications, and pay their vows to the Lord who dwelleth in Zion. At the same time, first the Greek and then the Roman conquerors overran the land; and from the time of Herod, not only were Greek artists and artizans to be seen at work in Palestine, but Greek colonies in no small numbers were also to be found. The combined influence of these circumstances had, in the time of Christ, brought about this peculiar condition of things in Palestine, that the Greek language was almost universally (ziemlich allgemein) understood, while the proper Jewish language was understood only by the strictly Jewish inhabitants; so that one may say, almost all the dwellers in Palestine understood Greek, but not all their own vernacular language."[1]

[1] Credner, Einleitung, § 75. Winer, in his *Realwörterbuch* (Art. Sprache), while upholding the prevalent idea that our Lord usually spoke in Aramaic,

All the points here mentioned admit, we believe, of satisfactory proof; and most of them, indeed, scarcely require any to those who are acquainted with the history of the period. Josephus testifies very clearly to the existence of numerous colonies of Greeks in Palestine, and to the commingling of these in many cities with the native Jews.[y] And Tacitus as well as Josephus informs us, that besides the influence which would thus naturally be exerted in favour of the Greek customs and language, the power of the monarch was at times specially put forth in the same direction. The Roman historian declares (Hist. lib. v., c. viii.), "Postquam Macedones præpotuere, rex Antiochus demere superstitionem, et *mores Græcorum dare* adnixus;" and the Jewish writer tells us (Antiq. xix. 7, 3) respecting Herod, the predecessor of Agrippa, that he plainly declared his partiality for the Greeks, and practically demonstrated this sentiment by loading them with favours, and greatly embellishing their cities, while an opposite course of conduct was followed with respect to the Jews. There are also, as has been shewn by the researches of Burckhardt and other Eastern travellers, inscriptions remaining on temples, gates, and other ancient public buildings in Palestine, which prove to us by ocular evidence at the present day the wide-spread and commanding influence possessed by the Greek tongue in that country before and at the commencement of the Christian era.

On the whole, then, we may conclude this Section with the words of the learned Vossius, which are quoted by Diodati, from the treatise "De Sybillinis oraculis," although, as will be observed,

(partly on *à priori* grounds, and partly on the occurrence of such passages as Mark v. 41, and Matt. xxvii. 46, which reasons will be fully examined in the following Section,) nevertheless admits the very wide extent to which Greek was known in Palestine. "Gewiss ist," he says, "dass die Juden, seit der seleucidischen Periode, zum grossen Theil griechisch verstanden." The translators of our English Bible observe, in their Preface, "The Greek tongue was well known and made familiar to *most inhabitants in Asia*, by reason of the conquests which there the Grecians had made, as also by the colonies which thither they had sent."

[y] Bell. Jud. ii. 18, 3, iii. 9; Antiq. xix. 6, 3; Vita Jos. § 12, etc.; 1 Macc. xii. 33, 34; 2 Macc. xii. 3, etc.

In proof of the result as stated above by Credner, see Matt. xxvii. 47, and Mark xv. 35, where the only *natural* interpretation of the words shows that, among some of the *Jews*, Hebrew was not then understood.

his language at the close is somewhat stronger than we deem it necessary to employ: "Ubicunque jam ab Alexandri Magni temporibus, Græci fuere domini, ibi etiam Græca prævaluit lingua, et *absurdum est unam excipere Judæam*, cum et Josephus et Machabæorum libri satis testentur quam prompti sub Græcis regibus fuerint Judæi in adsciscendis Græcorum moribus, adeo ut major pars Græci quam Judæi videri maluerint. Linguam Græcam, id est, linguam dominantium, etiam illi qui Græcos oderant, si intelligi et rebus suis vellent consulere addiscere cogebantur; ut in Ægypto, Asia, et reliqua Syria, ita quoque in Judæa, nulla præter Græcam audiebatur lingua."

## SECTION III.—PROOFS FROM THE WRITINGS OF THE NEW TESTAMENT THAT GREEK WAS THE PREVAILING LANGUAGE OF PALESTINE IN THE DAYS OF CHRIST AND HIS APOSTLES.

We now proceed to what has been announced as the principal object contemplated in this Chapter—the production of proof from the New Testament itself that Greek was the dominant language of Judæa at the commencement of our era, and was consequently the language, for the most part, employed by our Lord and his immediate followers.

In entering on this very important section of the argument, we may begin by remarking, that the *prima facie* evidence—that which results from a general survey of the New Testament from a purely literary point of view, is undeniably in favour of our proposition. For let the simple facts of the case be considered. Here we possess, in the volume known as the New Testament, a collection of writings, composed for the most part *by* Jews of Palestine, and primarily intended to some extent *for* Jews of Palestine, and all of them written (if we leave out of sight, in the meantime, the disputed original of St. Matthew's Gospel) in the Greek language. Now, what is the natural inference? Is it not that Greek must have been well known both to the writers and their readers, and that *it* was deemed the most fitting language at the time in which for Jews of Palestine both to impart and receive instruction? Such at least is the conclusion which would instantly be reached from the existence of similar facts in any other case. When we find that an ancient writer addressed his countrymen at large in a particular language, we naturally infer that both he and they were familiar with that language, and that it was chosen by him as the most suitable vehicle for conveying to them what he wished to communicate.

And why should we not draw the same inference with reference to the writers and readers of the New Testament? When we find the Galilean Peter taking up his pen and writing in Greek, why should we not suppose that Greek was the common language of Galilee? And when we find the author of the Epistle to the Hebrews writing to the Jews of Palestine[z] in Greek, how can we escape from the conclusion that they generally understood that language? There can be no doubt that the writer of the last-named epistle (suppose him to have been whom you will) was a learned Jew, well-skilled in Hebrew; his work itself bears ample evidence of that fact: and when, nevertheless, we find him writing to his countrymen in Greek, it seems necessary to conclude that the Greek language was well known to those whom he addressed, and that it was deemed by him the most suitable medium through which to convey to them his instructions. It is the weakest of all arguments to attempt to set aside these inferences by replying that the epistle in question was intended for the benefit of the whole Christian world, and was on that account written in Greek, and not in the ordinary language of those to

[z] "The Jews of Palestine;" for that it was to them this epistle was addressed is almost universally admitted. "This epistle," says Hug (Introd. ii. § 141), "as its plan, the actual character of its different parts, and almost every passage testify, was written for Jews; and, moreover, for such Jews as were minutely acquainted with the ceremonies of religious worship at Jerusalem, the temple service, and things connected therewith. True, this acquaintance might be possessed by every learned Jew; but a promiscuous collection of people (such as the author of the epistle certainly addressed) could not be supposed to possess it, unless they had opportunity to acquire it from actual and frequent observation. Chrysostom, therefore, is correct in his general view when he infers, simply from the knowledge previously requisite to understand the epistle, that it was written to Jews in Palestine." This was the unanimous opinion of the ancients, and to it the great majority of modern critics have adhered.

whom it was primarily sent. We willingly admit the universal, as well as particular design of the epistle: we gratefully acknowledge that it is fraught with most valuable lessons for Christians in our own, and in every age, no less than for the Christians of Palestine in the early days of the church. But still, it was to the Hebrew believers of those days that it was specially inscribed; it was for their benefit that it was ostensibly written: and however wide, therefore, the field which its divinely inspired contents might afterwards enrich, or however lasting might prove its value to the whole Christian church, we cannot suppose it to have been written in a language with which its original readers were not well acquainted; and that thus *their* interests, while professedly sought, were in reality cruelly and mockingly disregarded for the sake of others.

Two questions, then, instantly arise on the point under consideration, as soon as we give even the most cursory glance at the contents of the New Testament, and which seem to admit of only one answer. The first of these is, How could Palestinian Jews, like Peter, James, and John,—"unlettered and ignorant men," as they were called—men, certainly possessed of no advantages either of rank or education above the respectable labouring classes in Judæa—have written in Greek, unless that were the language which men in the humblest station naturally employed? And the second question is, How could it have been supposed by these writers that they would be understood by their countrymen in Palestine, unless it had been taken for granted that Greek was a language with which all Jews were then more or less familiar?

There is only one mode of escaping from the conclusion which follows from the first of these questions, and it has been had recourse to by some of the upholders of the Hebrew original of St. Matthew's Gospel. It is implied in the following words of Greswell: "If the Greek alone," he says, "would have sufficed every where out of Palestine as the vehicle of a popular address, what necessity for the gift of any other language? And if the Greek was understood even in Palestine, what necessity even there for the gift of that?"[a] It is thus supposed, that, although

[a] Harmony of the Gospels, i. 141.

Peter and James did not naturally use or understand Greek, yet by the gift of tongues they were supernaturally endowed with a knowledge of that language. But such a supposition is equally opposed to reason and Scripture. It is repugnant to the constitution and working of the human mind, and to all that is told us in, or may be inferred from, Scripture, as to the manner in which the Spirit of God operates upon it. He who has made us as we are, graciously and wisely accommodates his actings to that spiritual and intellectual nature he has imparted, and ever honours his own workmanship, as displayed in our mental habitudes and laws, by making use of these in the supernatural operations of his grace. Now, such a supposition as that of Greswell and others is utterly opposed to all that we know or can conceive of the mechanism and exercise of the human understanding. This has been stated by Mr. Alford in his notes on the second chapter of Acts, which contains an account of the miraculous gift of tongues. "I would not conceal," he says, "the difficulty which our minds find in conceiving a person supernaturally endowed with the power of speaking (and the same remark applies, of course, to writing) *ordinarily and consciously* a language which he has never learned. I believe that difficulty to be insuperable. Such an endowment would not only be contrary to the analogy of God's dealings, but, as far as I can see into the matter, self-contradictory, and therefore impossible. But there is no such contradiction, and, to my mind, no such difficulty, in conceiving a man to be moved to utterance of sounds dictated by the Holy Spirit." And this accordingly is the view of the gift of tongues which is now obtaining general adoption among all the best expositors of Scripture.

"The design of this gift," says Dr. Alexander, in his recent work on the Acts of the Apostles (i. 45), "was not merely to facilitate the preaching of the Gospel. It is *nowhere* historically mentioned as contributing to that result. Its necessity for that end was in a great measure superseded, at least within the Roman empire, by the general use of the Greek language. That it was not a permanent and universal knowledge of all the tongues spoken in the countries visited by the Apostles is inferred by some from xiv. 11, where the use of the vernacular language seems to be mentioned as an explanation of the tardiness with which Paul and

Barnabas rejected the idolatrous honours of the heathen Lycaonians. While the gift of tongues may, in particular emergencies, have answered this important purpose, it had other uses, even regarded as a transient or momentary inspiration. It served, like any other miracle, but with a special propriety and force, to prove the reality of an extraordinary spiritual influence, which might otherwise have been denied or doubted. And it served as a symbol to prefigure the vocation of the Gentiles, whose excision from the church or chosen people had been typified of old by a corresponding prodigy, the miraculous confusion of tongues at Babel. As the moral unity of mankind had been then lost, it was now to be restored by the preaching of the Gospel to all nations. To this historical connexion between diversities of language and the spiritual condition of the world, there seems to be allusion in the frequent use of the word *tongues* to designate nations. While the practical design of this gift, as an aid in preaching, would confine it to one sex and a small class of believers, its demonstrative and symbolical design made it equally appropriate to others."

It is manifest from this passage, that while Dr. Alexander expresses himself with his usual caution, he nevertheless inclines to that view of the miraculous gift of tongues, which alone, as stated above, we can regard as tenable. And Alford, with that definiteness of statement, which is one of the many valuable features in his Commentary, leaves no doubt on the minds of his readers as to the conclusion which he has formed. "Was this speaking in various languages," he asks, "a gift bestowed on the Disciples *for their use afterwards*, or was it a mere sign, their utterance being only as they were mouthpieces of the Holy Spirit? The latter seems certainly to have been the case. . . . If the first supposition be made, that the gift of speaking in various languages was bestowed on the Disciples for their after use in preaching the Gospel, we are, I think, running counter to the whole course of Scripture, and early patristic evidence on the subject. There is no trace whatever of such a power being possessed or exercised by the Apostles, or by those who followed them. I believe, therefore, the event related in our text to have been a sudden and powerful inspiration of the Holy Spirit, by which the disciples uttered, not of their own minds, but as mouthpieces of the Spirit, the praises of God in various languages, hitherto, and possibly at the time itself, unknown to them."

Whatever opinion may be formed on the last point referred to in this extract, it will, we think, be admitted by most modern critics, that both the facts of Scripture, the testimony of antiquity, and the nature of the case, lead us to the conclusion, that no language, hitherto unknown to the Apostles, was then communicated to them for ordinary use in their subsequent career, as preachers or as writers in the service of the Gospel. The miracle witnessed on the day of Pentecost, seems, from the narrative itself, to have had quite another object. And in those remains which have been preserved to us of the Apostles' discourses and writings, we find no traces of any such sudden or unnatural communication of knowledge. The Bible is throughout the most *natural* of all books. Every writer, while under the influence of the Holy Ghost, is yet permitted fully to exhibit his own idiosyncrasies, to make use of his own acquirements, and to write in his own style. While the whole is the Word of God, the several parts are as manifestly the productions of different men. And this not only imparts to it a charm, which a uniformity of thought or style would necessarily have lacked, but, as every one knows, serves a highly important purpose in the vital question of its authenticity. In all thoroughly genuine and unaffected works, the *man* appears in the *author:* the book reflects the character, and, as it were, embodies the soul of him who composed it. And, as every reader must feel, this is strikingly characteristic of the Bible. Its human authors seem truly to have realized the remarkable expression by which some simple tribes have described the art of composition, and to have *pressed their souls on the paper* on which they wrote. Now, this is quite compatible with the doctrine, that they were supernaturally guided in the use of their natural powers, so that all their writings, while displaying their special characters, yet possess in common the attribute of Divine inspiration; but how it could be consistent with the miraculous impartation to any of them of a new language for ordinary use, seems impossible to conceive. Such a notion introduces the idea of the factitious and unreal, and appears quite repugnant to that naturalness which is so marked a characteristic of the Bible. The opinion, indeed, of Greswell and others, that the *Greek* in which the Apostles spoke and wrote was directly conveyed to them from heaven, involves so many difficulties, and presents such glaring improbabilities, if it does not even imply utter contradictions, that we do not think any sober and reflecting mind can entertain it. We must therefore conclude, that when Peter, James, and John, spoke or wrote in the Greek tongue, they just naturally made use of that language with which they were best acquainted, and which they knew to be most fitted for the purpose designed to be accomplished.

But, then, this conclusion immediately draws after it another. If Peter and James naturally made use of the Greek language, that language must have been known to all classes in the community. These first Disciples of Jesus were taken from the lower ranks among the people. They had, no doubt, previous to their call to the Apostleship, received the elements of an ordinary education; and there can be no question, that during the years of their intercourse with Jesus, great additions were made to their intellectual vigour and attainments. But still, if *they*, humble fishermen of Galilee, understood Greek to such an extent as naturally to write in it, the inference is inevitable, that *that language must have been generally known and used among the people.*[b]

The same conclusion instantly follows from a consideration of the second question which was proposed, viz., How it could have been imagined that writings in Greek would be understood by the inhabitants of Palestine, and how they should accordingly have been addressed by the Apostles in that language? Even supposing that an acquaintance with Greek was supernaturally conveyed to the writers of the New Testament, it cannot be supposed that their readers were supernaturally endowed to understand it. And, as it is impossible to believe that such an Epistle

[b] Or, at least, among the *lower* orders. It has usually been said, that Greek, if known at all in Palestine, must have been limited to the higher ranks; but the inference from what is stated above, is exactly the reverse. This has been seen by Credner, who, on far better grounds, certainly, than those on which the opposite opinion rests, writes thus: "So geschah es, dass in Palästina die griechische Sprache vorzüglich unter den niedern Ständen der eingebornen Juden heimisch war, ohne dass sie darum den Uebrigen unbekannt bleiben konnte." Einl. § 76.

as that of St. James to the twelve tribes, or that of St. Paul (or whoever else may have been the author) to the Hebrews, would have been addressed to them in Greek, unless they had been able easily to read it, we must conclude that the Jews generally, *in* Palestine, as well as *out* of it, then possessed a familiar acquaintance with that language.

It is, indeed, a striking proof of the wisdom of God, that the Scriptures of the New Testament should have been given to mankind in a language then understood by the world at large, and not in a dialect like the Aramæan, which was intelligible only within a very limited territory. But it is to blot and disparage that wisdom, if it be supposed necessary, that in order to carry its purpose into effect, the persons who were originally addressed had to be overlooked, and that by writing to them in Greek their interests were to some extent sacrificed, while those of the world at large were consulted. Yet this is the conclusion to which those must come, who hold that Hebrew was, on any account, the proper language of religious address among the Jews in the days of Christ and his Apostles. The Hebrews of Palestine were addressed in Greek by the writer of that Epistle which specially bears their name; and this, it is said, was done, not because that was the most fitting language in which to address them,—the contrary is maintained,—but for the sake of the rest of the world. Such a notion seems too preposterous to require refutation. It is plain, that had the fact been as supposed, the Epistle in question must rather have irritated than edified those who received it. And if it be said, as it often is, that St. Matthew wrote his Gospel in Hebrew, in order to conciliate the prejudices of his countrymen by relating the Gospel-history in their own language, how much more necessary was it, that in an Epistle like that to the Hebrews, which strikes at the root of all that was peculiarly Jewish, this means of propitiating and pleasing them should not be neglected! And yet the Epistle in question was written in the *Greek*, and not the Hebrew language.[c]

[c] The difficulty here suggested, applies, of course, with double force to those who imagine that Hebrew was the common language of Palestine at the time referred to, and yet are inclined to believe that the Gospel of St. Matthew was written in Greek. This seems to be the case with Dr. Fair-

But, on the other hand, if our supposition be admitted, that Greek was then the fitting language of popular address *in Palestine*, as in the rest of the civilized world, how illustriously does the wisdom of God shine forth! He had by his providence, gradually brought the world into such a condition, that without any violent interference on his part, there was existing on the earth, at the commencement of our era, a language which was known both to Jews and Gentiles. And thus, without any miraculous operations, and without any preference of the interests of one nation to those of another, the Greek language was adopted as that of the New Testament, the language in which the Scriptures of the latter dispensation were naturally, as well as most fittingly, composed.

Looking, then, at that part of the New Testament, which has as yet been specially noticed—the Epistles, is not the natural inference to be drawn from the data which it furnishes, just that which has been stated? And *why seek any other?* Why perplex and confound such a simple case, as that of men writing naturally in a language which they themselves understood, to others in a language which they understood also, by supposing that the writers were led to compose their works in a language which they

bairn, as his views are brought out in his recent "Hermeneutical Manual." He maintains very strongly, the idea that the Aramaic was then the ordinary language of Palestine. We shall have occasion afterwards to refer to some of his arguments in defence of this opinion, but meanwhile we would suggest the following question to his consideration. *If Aramaic was then the common language of Palestine, how comes it to pass that both the Gospel of St. Matthew, and the Epistle to the Hebrews, were addressed to the natives of that country in Greek?* It is no answer to say, as he does in another connexion (p. 11), that the Jewish Christians, "having in the first instance enjoyed many opportunities of becoming personally acquainted with the facts of gospel-history, and enjoying afterwards the ministry of Apostles and Evangelists, who were perfectly cognizant of the whole, were in a manner independent of any written records." The *fact* nevertheless remains, that these natives of Palestine *did* receive written records, and those, as he believes, in the Greek language. They were certainly specially addressed by the writer of the Epistle to the Hebrews; and Dr. F. departs from all consent, both ancient and modern, if he does not admit that St. Matthew wrote his Gospel with a special reference to his Jewish countrymen. How, then, comes it to pass, if Aramaic was the prevailing language of the country, that both these documents were written in Greek?

themselves did *not* naturally understand, and to send these to men who could not easily, perhaps not at all, comprehend what was thus addressed to them?

And, if we now glance at the other great division of the New Testament books—the Gospels, do we find any ground for supposing that these merely contain *translations* of the words which our Lord employed? Is there a single hint to that effect given by any of the writers? Do they not, on the contrary, express themselves exactly as they would have done, supposing they had meant to report to us the very language which was made use of by the Saviour? Their constant formula is, "Jesus *said*," or, "he spoke these *words*," and that, whether it happens to be Greek or Hebrew which they record as the language that was uttered. There is no hint, *e. g.* that St. John *translated* the word which Jesus employed, when he tells us that our Lord exclaimed on the cross, τετέλεσται, any more than when we are informed by another Evangelist that he cried, Ἐλωῒ, Ἐλωῒ, λαμμᾶ σαβαχθανὶ; but in both these, and other similar cases, the natural impression produced on our mind is, that the very language is reported to us, which then actually proceeded out of the Saviour's mouth.

A very strange mode of reasoning, as it appears to us, has prevailed with respect to those occasional Aramaic expressions, which are inserted in the Gospels as having been employed by Christ. It has been argued, that the occurrence of such terms now and then in the reports which have been preserved to us of our Lord's discourses, *proves* that he generally made use of the Syro-Chaldaic language,[d] and that accordingly, it was in these

[d] Thus, among a multitude of others, the Abbé Migne, in his valuable "Encyclopédie Theologique." He says, (vol. iii. Art. Matthieu), "Quelque commune que fût la langue grecque dans la Palestine, et quoiq'elle pût être la langue vulgaire de certaines villes de ce pays, où le nombre des Grecs était plus grand que celui des autres habitants, il est certain toutefois que le commun des Juifs parlait plus ordinairement ce qu'ils appelaient hébreu, mais qui était plutôt un syriaque et un chaldéen mêlé de quelque mots hébreux. On le voit *par l'Evangile meme*, qui nous a conservé quelques mots hébreux que J. C. a prononcés, et qu'on ne rapporte pas comme une chose singulière, en sorte qu'on en puisse conclure qu'il n'en a point prononcé d'autres: il paraît, au contraire, que c'était son langage ordinaire."

few instances only that we have examples of the very words which he employed. But such a conclusion rests upon a manifest *petitio principii:* there is not the least foundation furnished for it in the evangelic narrative. The writers never hint that they are giving the words of Jesus more exactly when they report Hebrew than when they report Greek. On the contrary, as has been said, the very same mode of expression is made use of by them, whether it be the one language or the other that our Lord is represented as employing; and to say, therefore, that the occurrence, here and there, of an Aramaic word or phrase proves that he habitually made use of that dialect, is simply to *assume* the point in question, and to mistake for a sound and valid argument, what is in reality a foregone conclusion.

Moreover, if it be maintained that the Aramaic was the language which Christ generally employed, the question instantly occurs, why we have a few such words, and a few only, preserved to us as having been used by him on rare occasions. On the supposition that he spoke usually in Greek, these words, we believe, come in naturally enough as exceptions to the general rule, and are specially inserted as such, just as in the reported discussions of Cicero, we often find a few Greek terms introduced; and as in our own language, a French or German expression may every now and then occur. But if, on the other hand, it be supposed that Christ really for the most part made use of the Aramaic, so that *the Greek* was the exception and not the rule in his discourses, it seems impossible to give any satisfactory, or even tolerable explanation, of the manner in which the few Aramaic words found in the Gospels are introduced. They certainly *appear* to be brought in as exceptional to his usual practice; and when regarded in that light, their occurrence can cause little difficulty, even although no evident reason may be found for his use of the Aramaic on these particular occasions. But, when the opposite opinion is maintained, and when these words are looked on as really specimens of his ordinary language, there is no principle of reason which can be suggested as likely to have guided the evangelists in their preservation and insertion. The most improbable, and even mutually contradictory, explanations of this matter, have been offered by those who imagine that our Lord generally made use of Hebrew, as will be plain from the following examples.

Dr. Pfannkuche, having stated that in the well-known passages (Matt. xxvii. 46; Mark xv. 34; v. 41; vii. 34), we have "some fragments of Christ's speeches preserved in the original language," adds in a note, "We can only *conjecture* why these passages of our Greek Gospels, which otherwise always give Jesus' speeches and sayings in Greek, contain only a few words of the original text. In the two first quoted passages, as it seems, the original expression is inserted, *because* thereby light is thrown upon the circumstance immediately after mentioned,—that Jesus, according to the supposition of some by-standers, cried for help from Elias. In the two latter passages, where the preservation of the words of the original seems to be rather *accidental than intentional*, the translator may have been in the same predicament as the authors of the Alexandrine version, who now and then did retain, probably *from mere inadvertence*, a single Hebrew word," etc.[e]

It is needless to notice the weakness of this explanation, if, indeed, it deserves the name of explanation. The dishonour which it does to the character of our Gospels, as written by *intelligent*, not to say *inspired* men, must be obvious to every reader.

But other solutions of the difficulty have been suggested. Thus Dean Trench, says in his "Notes on the Miracles" (p. 186), "St. Mark gives us, probably from the lips of Peter, the very words which the Lord spake in the very language wherein he uttered them,—*Talitha Cumi*,—no doubt as having something *especially solemn* in them, as he does the *Ephphatha* on another occasion." Compare with this the language of Dr. Fairbairn, in his "Hermeneutical Manual" (p. 8):—"When our Lord appears in the

[e] On this passage, the English translator of Pfannkuche (p. 46), while favourable to the general view maintained by his author, remarks, with his usual candour, "The translator is not much disposed to dispute the author's general position with regard to the language of Palestine at the time of Christ; but he thinks it but fair to observe, that the proof here drawn from Christ's speeches is *excessively weak*." He then goes on to show this, and adds,—"After all, Dr. Pfannkuche here only *presupposes*, and has not *proved*, that the Greek Gospels are only translations." "*Ex uno disce omnes;*" it has been *supposition*, and not *proof*, which has been characteristic of all that have maintained the views of Pfannkuche on this matter.

attitude of addressing any one *very familiarly*, or of giving or adopting designations for common use, he is represented as speaking in Aramaic; as when he said to the daughter of Jairus, *Talitha Cumi*, and to the dumb man, *Ephphatha;* or when he referred to the terms commonly employed among the people, such as *raka*, *rabbi*, *corban;* when he applied to his Disciples such epithets as *Cephas*, *Barjona*, *Boanerges;* or when on the cross He exclaimed, 'Eli, Eli, lama sabachthani.'"

Now it will be here noticed, in the first place, that the reasons assigned by these two eminent writers respectively for our Lord's employment of such words as *Talitha Cumi* or *Ephphatha*, are utterly contradictory to one another. Dr. Trench says, that St. Mark gives us these words because there was something "especially solemn in them;" and Dr. Fairbairn tells us, that our Lord's Aramaic expressions are preserved when he "appears in the attitude of addressing any one very familiarly." It is not easy to see how the especially *solemn* and the very *familiar* could be mingled in the selfsame utterance, and thus the one explanation refutes the other, and we are still left without any explanation at all.

Moreover, it is manifest that if we take the two different solutions separately, neither of them furnishes us with any satisfactory account of the matter. There are many specially solemn occasions on which our Lord's words are given in *Greek*,—such as those majestic terms preserved in St. Mark only, by which He soothed the tempestuous lake, and that mighty utterance of power which, as St. John informs us, brought forth from his grave the sleeping Lazarus. Dr. Fairbairn's explanation, again, is not only insufficient, but utterly unsuitable to the circumstances. We can see how, in the language of Trench, the expressions referred to may justly be designated "solemn;" but how they can, in any sense, be reckoned "familiar," we are at a loss to conceive. And surely it must have been a great oversight in Dr. Fairbairn, when he classes with very familiar utterances the most awful words, perhaps, which ever passed human lips—even the lips of the God-man, many as were the impressive words He spoke—that cry of deepest pathos, and to us inconceivable significance, "My God, my God, why hast thou forsaken me?"

But now it may be asked, Can any explanation of the occurrence of these Aramaic expressions be given, *on the theory which we maintain*, that our Lord spoke generally in Greek, and only now and then in Hebrew? In answer to this question, it seems almost sufficient to repeat the statement which has been already made of the relation which we conceive to have existed between the two languages. Let it be remembered, that we admit the simultaneous existence in Palestine, at the date referred to, of both the Aramaic and Greek, the former language no doubt, in many respects, subordinate to the latter, but still *the mother-tongue of the whole native population;* and how natural the supposition, that in such circumstances, our Lord should sometimes have found it expedient to depart from His usual practice, and make use of the vernacular language of the country! Occasions may easily be imagined, on which He would find it suitable to do so; just as a public teacher in many countries at the present day, while generally employing the language of literature there prevalent, would find it edifying and instructive, to introduce occasionally some words from the common language of the people.[f] The necessity for explanation then, is, on our hypothesis, much less stringent than on the opposite. If it be supposed that our Lord spoke almost always in Aramaic, it seems truly singular, that so very few of His expressions in that language should have been preserved by the Evangelists, and that no hint should have been given that they were then specially reporting to us the very words which He employed. If, on the other hand, Greek was the language which He *generally* made use of, and if, accordingly, His discourses are

[f] The following incident may be given in illustration of what is stated above. On one occasion Dr. Chalmers, the great Scottish preacher, was labouring with all the power of his earnest and eloquent lips to convey to a poor woman whom he had visited an acquaintance with the nature of *faith*. He tried to represent his meaning under every form of speech which the English language afforded, but in vain. There was still no sign of answering intelligence on the part of his hearer; when at last, deserting the English tongue altogether, he cried, "Just *lippen* to Him." This word "lippen" is the common Scotch expression for "confide" or "trust," and it was no sooner uttered than the idea wished to be conveyed was apprehended. What all the illustrative power of Chalmers failed to effect by means of *English*, was at once effected by his use of this *Scotch* expression; and yet it could surely never be argued from this that his addresses generally *were*, or *should have been*, delivered in the latter language.

reported to us almost *verbatim* by the writers of the Gospels, there is no ground for surprise that an Aramaic expression should now and then occur, although we may not perceive the reason why that language was then employed by our Lord, or why its employment was particularly noticed by the Evangelists. But we are willing to go further than this. We think some reasons may be gathered, from the special circumstances in which the few Aramaic words preserved in the Gospels were made use of, why that language, rather than the Greek, should have been employed; and why its employment should have been expressly recorded in the narrative.

The first passage calling for explanation, is Mark v. 41, which is thus rendered in our English version: "He took the damsel by the hand, and said unto her, Talitha cumi; which is, being interpreted, Damsel (I say unto thee), arise." Now, on the supposition that *Greek* was our Lord's usual form of address, we think a very good and satisfactory reason can be perceived for the exception which is here particularly noted. The language which He employed, was, of course, immaterial, so far as the result was concerned: the designed effect would have followed, whatever words, or although no words, had been made use of; and, as the translator of Pfannkuche has remarked, "whether the people, standing by, understood them or not, was of no moment." It must, then, have been from considerations connected with the *damsel herself*, that our Lord's choice of a language on this occasion was determined: and we venture to propose the following, as sufficient to account for His having made use of the Aramaic. The person on whom the miracle was performed was of tender years, and on that account, probably, was not yet very familiar with the Greek. At any rate it was to her, as to every native Jew, a foreign language; and it was to the Hebrew that her ears from infancy had been accustomed. How beautifully accordant, then, with the character of Him, whose heart was tenderness itself, that now, as He bent over the lifeless frame of the maiden, and breathed that life-giving whisper into her ear, it should have been in the loved and familiar accents of her mother-tongue! Although dead and insensible the moment before the words were uttered, yet ere the sound of them passed away, there was life and sensibility within her. And does not every reader therefore perceive, in the thoughtful tenderness of the act, a most sufficient reason why it was in Hebrew, and not in Greek, that our Lord addressed her? And, do we not also discover a cause, why the fact of His having done so should be specially noticed by the Evangelist? Are we not thus furnished with a fresh and affecting example of our Saviour's graciousness? and do we not feel that St. Mark—the most minutely-descriptive of all the Evangelists—deserves our gratitude for having taken pains to record it? Softly and sweetly must the tones of that loving voice, speaking in the language of her childhood, have fallen on the sleeping spirit of the maiden: and by words of tenderness, no less than words of power, was she thus recalled to life and happiness.

Equally natural, as we deem it, is the explanation, which may, on our hypothesis, be given of our Lord's use of the Aramaic language, in the case of the deaf and dumb man, recorded in Mark vii. 32-37. At ver. 34, we read that the Saviour, having gone through those impressive preliminaries by which this miracle was preceded, said unto the man, "Ephphatha." And "straightway," it is added, "his ears were opened, and the string of his tongue was loosed, and he spake plain." Now here, as before, our Lord's choice of a particular language could only have been determined by *a regard to the man himself*. And, as the slightest additional reason for His selection of one language rather than another, must have been quite enough for Him who never violated propriety, in even the lowest degree, we may be satisfied if we can discover, in the peculiar circumstances of this man, the least probable ground for the preference here given by our Lord, to the Aramaic over the Greek. Supposing, then, as many commentators do, that the man had been hitherto entirely deaf and speechless, it appears to us fitting and proper, that the very first sounds which fell upon his ears, and the first which his liberated tongue would naturally attempt to imitate, should be those of the vernacular language of his country. So far as respected the power of articulate speech, this man was as a child. He had to *learn to speak*, as the infant gradually does; and while Jesus removed the impediments which had hitherto prevented this, He did not, of course, convey to the man a miraculous acquaintance with any language. The faculty was imparted, but it had to be used by the man himself, in order to lead to those attainments of which till now he had been destitute; and dealing with him as with a child (which in regard to speech he was), the Saviour kindly and graciously addressed him in the mother-tongue of his native land. But another view may be taken of this man's case; and that, which with Trench and others, we prefer. It would seem, from some expressions made use of in the narrative, that the man was not *entirely* destitute of the power of speech, nor of course, in that case, of hearing. He is said to have been μογιλάλος, and, after the miracle was performed, to have spoken ὀρθῶς; both of which terms appear to imply, that he had previously been able, in a measure, to speak and hear, though very defectively. And, on this supposition, it is, perhaps, still more easy to see why our Lord addressed him in Aramaic, since that was the only language of which it was likely that he could have had any knowledge. The man was dealt with throughout as an intelligent being; the various signs employed doubtless conveyed a meaning to his mind; and when at last the decisive word was spoken, it was in the highest degree proper, that *that also* should be intelligible to him: it was therefore uttered in a language which alone, in his afflicted circumstances, he could have learned at all to understand—the mother-tongue of his native country.[g]

In the only other remarkable instance recorded in the Gospels, of our Lord's use of Hebrew instead of Greek,—His cry upon the cross,—the reason for His having chosen the one language in preference to the other, must be obvious to every reader. His thoughts naturally reverted, in that hour of suffering, to the very words which His illustrious type had used in the time of his distress,—words on which the Saviour's mind had, no doubt, often before pondered, and words, therefore, which then spontaneously

[g] I am quite prepared to find that the above explanations will appear to some readers far-fetched and fanciful. But let it be remembered that *no account whatever* can be given of these Aramaic expressions on the supposition that our Lord usually spoke in that language. Even, therefore, although the explanations we have offered appear utterly insufficient, we are still (to say the least) in no worse a position than those on the other side. And, we are not without hope that some will deem our position better.

rose to His lips in their original form, as He experienced the hidings of his Father's countenance.

And, on the hypothesis that our Lord spoke for the most part in Greek, we can also naturally account for those isolated and occasional Hebrew words which are found in His discourses. The Aramaic had, of course, no small influence upon the Greek of the country, and necessarily insinuated many of its idioms and expressions into the co-existing language. Hence the occurrence of such words as, *Amen*, *corban*, *raka*, etc.; of such designations as *Cephas*, *Boanerges*, etc.; and of such phrases as πρόσωπον λαμβάνειν, γεύεσθαι θανάτου, etc. It seems no easy matter, on the supposition that our Lord generally made use of Hebrew, to account for the retaining of such words as have been mentioned, *in their original form*, while His language is for the most part translated; whereas, on our theory, that the substance of His discourse was Greek, nothing could be more natural, or, indeed, inevitable, than that such Aramaic words and phrases should from time to time occur, and be preserved.

It appears, then, from a general survey of the New Testament, that there is every reason to conclude, that Greek was commonly known and used in Palestine, in the days of Christ and His Apostles; that *that* accordingly was the language which He and they usually employed; and that, while both the Master and His Disciples occasionally made use of the Aramaic dialect, such an occurrence was quite exceptional to their general practice, and is, therefore, specially noticed in the evangelic history.

We may now proceed to support our argument, by a reference to some particular incidents and passages in the New Testament. Here, we shall only notice a few which seem most plainly and directly to bear upon the subject, and shall make no attempt to consider or apply the whole.

Let our readers, then, reflect on the statements made in the "Acts of the Apostles," in connexion with the Day of Pentecost. There are several points to be noticed in the narrative, as serving to confirm our proposition, that Greek was then familiarly known to almost all Jews, whether dwelling *in* or *beyond* Palestine. The sacred historian tells us (ii. 5-11),—"And there were dwelling at Jerusalem, Jews, devout men, out of every nation under heaven.

. . . And they were all amazed, and marvelled, saying one to another, Behold, are not all these which speak Galileans? And how hear we every man in our own tongue, wherein we were born? Parthians, and Medes, and Elamites, and the dwellers in Mesopotamia, and in Judea, and Cappadocia, in Pontus, and Asia, Phrygia, and Pamphylia, in Egypt, and in the parts of Libya about Cyrene, and strangers of Rome, Jews and proselytes, Cretes and Arabians, we do hear them speak in our tongues the wonderful works of God." It is plain, we think, that the sacred historian here means to convey to us the idea, that the various representatives of the different nations then assembled in Jerusalem, did all hear themselves addressed in their own vernacular language. In some cases, perhaps, there were only differences of dialect among them; but at any rate, each nation was addressed in that which was deemed its own peculiar tongue. We believe, in spite of all the efforts which have been made by critics, both at home and abroad, to explain away the miracle, that if the fact just mentioned is not implied in the words of the writer, it is impossible to convey it by means of any words whatever. But at the same time, we think it equally plain from the narrative, that it was not for the purpose of enabling them to proclaim to these people the way of salvation, that the Apostles were thus endowed with the power of addressing them all in their own proper dialect. This was previously shown from the nature of the case, and from the facts of subsequent Apostolic history; but it also appears, from the point now specially soliciting our attention, that all these different tribes did, in truth, *possess a common language.* Two facts recorded in the narrative seem to make this undeniable. It appears first, from the incidental remark of the historian, that they all expressed astonishment among themselves, on account of the wonder which had just been witnessed. "They were all amazed," we are told, "and marvelled, *saying one to another*, Behold, are not all these which speak Galileans?" Now it seems a fair and necessary inference from this, that they all possessed a common language. Two men of the *same* nation *would* not thus have expressed their mutual wonder, since, in *their case*, there would have been no ground for it; and two men of *different* nations *could* not have expressed such wonder, *unless* they had possessed a common medium of communication. It is plain, then, that in addition to the knowledge of their own proper language or dialect, which the various nations possessed, they must also all have known Greek,—the world's language,—and thus been able to hold intercourse with one another.

But again, the same conclusion is derived from the fact afterwards stated, or, at least, clearly implied, that Peter addressed the whole multitude promiscuously in one language, and that they all understood him. His sermon which immediately followed the scene just described *must* have been delivered in the Greek language. Had he spoken in Hebrew, he would have been intelligible to only the merest fraction of his hearers; but as it was proved by the result—the conversion of no less than three thousand—that they had all understood him, it is plain that he must have used a form of speech familiar to them all,—and that could only be the Greek language. There can be no doubt whatever that both the native and foreign Jews were simultaneously addressed on this occasion. This appears very plainly among other proofs, from the exordium of the Apostle. He begins his address thus: "Ye men of Judea (*Ἄνδρες Ἰουδαῖοι*) and all ye that dwell at Jerusalem (*καὶ οἱ κατοικοῦντες Ἱερουσαλὴμ ἅπαντες*),"—and by these different appellations he can only mean, as is agreed by all critics, the native Jews who were regularly resident in Jerusalem, and the temporary sojourners from other countries. Here, then, we have a clear instance of a Jew of Palestine addressing, among others, Jews of Palestine in the *Greek language*, and so understood by them that many repented and believed; from which facts the inference is surely manifest that Greek was then thoroughly familiar to the natives of that country, and was regarded as a most fitting medium by which to convey to them religious instruction.

The proposition we announced has now been so clearly proved, that it seems almost needless to seek further arguments in its support.[h] As introductory, however, to some notice of the objections

[h] Many other passages might have been noticed above, but a multiplication of proofs would only tend to embarrass our argument. We may here, however, simply refer to some additional considerations. In John xii. 20, we read that some *Greeks* sought to be introduced to Jesus; and if, as is probable, their desire was granted, He undoubtedly spoke to them in their own lan-

usually brought against it, we shall here bring forward another passage which is thought to tell against us, but which when examined will be found to testify strongly in our favour. We refer to the statement made by Paul (Acts xxvi. 14) in giving an account of his conversion: "And when we were all fallen to the ground, I heard a voice speaking unto me and saying in the Hebrew tongue, Saul, Saul, why persecutest thou me?" Dr. Pfannkuche imagines that he here finds an argument against the common use of Greek in Palestine, since the Saviour is represented in this passage as speaking in the *Hebrew* language. "By Hebrew," the translator of Pfannkuche remarks, "the author no doubt means that we are to understand modern Hebrew or Aramaic." But how little the passage so understood can avail him will be plain from the criticism of his own translator, which is as follows: "The translator cannot help observing that Paul, being a learned Jew, would have understood ancient Hebrew as well; and if Jesus had spoken to him in the language of the country, there seemed little occasion for the narrator to specify that He had addressed him in that language. All his hearers would expect nothing else than that the language of the country had been used, unless the Apostle had told them something to the contrary; from which it seems to follow that Paul on this occasion was addressed in *ancient* Hebrew." We are obliged to the translator on this and several other occasions for pointing out to us the weakness of his author's position; but we must here express our conviction of the equal weakness of his own. It is quite true, as he remarks,

guage. His conversations with Pilate also were certainly conducted either by means of Greek or Latin, and far more probably in the former language. And "how," asks Hug, "did He address a mixed assemblage collected from different countries and cities? How did He address proselytes and pagans, *e. g.*, at Gadara? What language did He speak in the region of Tyre and Sidon, where the Syrophenician Greek woman entered into conversation with him? and what in Decapolis, which consisted of Greek cities, such as Philadelphia, Gerasa, Gadara, Hippos, and Pella?" It is certain that Greek *must* have been used by Christ on all such occasions, and therefore also certain that Dr. Fairbairn understates the case, at the least, when he says (Hermeneut. Man. p. 10) that "it may be admitted as perfectly possible, perhaps even probable," that our Lord and his immediate disciples "*sometimes*" made use of the Greek language.

that Paul would never have thought of particularly noticing the fact that Christ addressed him in Hebrew, had that been the common language of the country; but to attempt to escape from this difficulty by supposing that the Saviour then spoke in *ancient* instead of *modern* Hebrew, is still farther to embarrass the subject. The expression employed in the original is, Ἑβραΐδι διαλέκτῳ; and the same phrase occurs in other two places (xxi. 40, and xxii. 2), in both which it is interpreted by common consent as denoting Aramaic or modern Hebrew. It would then be the height of caprice to imagine that, in the present passage, it means not modern but ancient Hebrew; and the same rendering must evidently be given it in all the three places in which it occurs. Dr. Davidson justly remarks (Introd. i. 43) that "the opinion of Diodati that τῇ Ἑβραΐδι διαλέκτῳ (in xxii. 2) means ancient Hebrew, which the people who listened to Paul did not at all understand, though they allowed him to proceed for a time in his address, is so preposterous as to require no remark;" and if not so absurd in the present instance, the proposed rendering is at any rate equally capricious and untenable. How, then, shall we escape from the dilemma—how avoid the difficulty both of Pfannkuche and his translator, the one of whom makes the Apostle utter an unmeaning statement, and the other of whom attaches an unwarranted meaning to his words? The way is plain—*Greek*, and not *Hebrew*, was the common language of the country; and the Apostle, therefore, mentions it as something singular and striking that he was on this occasion addressed by the Saviour in Aramaic instead of the usual Greek, which might have been expected to be employed.

And thus we are led to notice another passage which is often referred to with great confidence as militating against our proposition. It is in Acts xxii. 2, where we read that "when the Jews heard that Paul spake to them in the Hebrew tongue they kept the more silence," "giving," as has been argued (Fairbairn and Davidson) "the more earnest heed to him as addressing them through a medium which was at once intelligible and congenial to their minds." Now, it has often been remarked, and is indeed evident to every reader of the narrative, that the Jews on this occasion expected to be addressed in another language than

Hebrew—the Greek of course—and were prepared intelligently to listen to such an address, a fact which proves at least their familiarity with that language. But then, it is said, they were better pleased to be spoken to in Hebrew; and hence it is argued that *that* was the most fitting language for a public instructor to employ. But such a notion is opposed to indisputable facts. We need only remember that Peter addressed the mixed assemblage at Jerusalem on the day of Pentecost in Greek, and that the multitude on this occasion expected to be addressed in that language, in order to see that Hebrew was *not the ordinary* medium of communication employed by public speakers or instructors. Why then did the Apostle now make choice of it, and why were the Jews so agreeably surprised on being addressed in it? Evidently, as it appears to us, from the special circumstances in which, relatively to his auditors, the Apostle was then placed. In the previous chapter we find that a great uproar had been excited among the Jews on account of his fancied opposition to all that they deemed most sacred. On perceiving him in the temple, some Jews of Asia had cried out, saying, "Men of Israel, help! This is the man that teacheth all men every where against the people, and the law, and this place; and further brought *Greeks* also into the temple, and hath polluted this holy place." Now, such being the nature of the suspicions with which the minds of the Jews were filled against him, nothing was more fitted to win for him a patient hearing, if that were possible, than at once to commence his address to them in their own vernacular language. His adoption of the Hebrew tongue was an instant witness in his favour. It proved that he was not so utterly estranged from all that was peculiarly Jewish as his enemies had represented; and no sooner, accordingly, had the sound of the old language been heard from his lips than the prepossessions against him lost much of their force, and there was manifested a greater disposition to hear him patiently. There can be no doubt that, prevalent as the Greek tongue then was in Palestine, the Jews, like any other nation, would be pleased, on such an occasion as the present, when their national prejudices were specially excited, to listen to the accents of their ancestral tongue. St. Paul, with that consummate wisdom and prudence which characterised him, now adapted himself to that most natural feeling; to the Jew he now became as a Jew, just as formerly at Athens he had, for the same end, become as a Greek to the Greek, and expressed himself in the language and style of an accomplished Grecian.

Some passages in Josephus are commonly referred to in connexion with this question. After a careful consideration of these, they appear to us too ambiguous to have much weight either on the one side or the other. We are inclined to believe, in opposition to Diodati, and in agreement with Dr. Davidson, that, by *πάτριος γλώσσῃ* (Bell. Jud. Procem.), the Jewish writer means the Hebrew, while by the words *ξένη καὶ ἀλλοδαπὴ διάλεκτος*, employed in another passage (Antiq. Procem.) he denotes the Greek. Our argument does by no means require us to deny this, as we have again and again freely admitted that to all native Jews the Hebrew was still their mother-tongue, though even in that respect, we believe, the Greek was almost able to contest with it the supremacy.[1] And, while accepting the explanation of Davidson in the passage referred to, rather than that of Diodati, it must at the same time be confessed that the view of the latter acquires not a little plausibility from the words of Josephus on another occasion. In his "Wars" (v. 2, 1), he tells us that Titus "pitched his camp at that valley which the Jews in *their own tongue* call 'the valley of thorns.'" (*Ἀκανθῶν Αὐλῶνα.*) Every one sees, as Diodati observes, that these words are pure Greek; and if, on this occasion, Josephus did not translate the name of the place from Hebrew into Greek, which seems contrary to his usual practice, we have his express authority for styling Greek, in a peculiar dialect, the then prevailing language of his country.

With regard to the other passage usually quoted from the "Antiquities" (xx. 11, 2), it is still more difficult to fix the exact meaning of the historian's words. Diodati supposes him here to refer to those efforts which he had made to translate his Jewish Antiquities into classical Greek. And it seems impossible to deny that the writer's words admit of this explanation. The phrase *πάτριος συνήθεια*, which he employs, certainly does not of neces-

[1] Lightfoot says on this point, and his authority in such a matter is second to none:—"The Jews (of that period) do well near acknowledge it (the Greek) for their mother-tongue even in Judæa."—Works, by Pitman, xi. 25.

sity mean "native *language*," but may, at least as naturally, be interpreted as referring to the mode of pronouncing Greek then common in Palestine. It is certain, moreover, that Josephus affected to write in a *classical* style. He seems to have prided himself on his attainments in this respect, and it is doubtful how far he would have acknowledged such a Hebraistic work as St. Matthew's Gospel as being, in his sense of the word, written in Greek at all. He complains, in the passage under consideration, that those who devoted themselves to the study of languages, and who *sought to acquire an elegant style*, were in little honour among his countrymen; and this complaint is quite in accordance with the opinion that he is throughout the paragraph speaking of the endeavours which he had made not to write in Greek, but in *pure and classical Greek*.[k] Altogether, his statements appear to us so ambiguous, that little importance can be attached to them either on the one side or the other.

It has, moreover, been objected that there is no plain or probable evidence of the Septuagint translation having ever been used in the synagogues of Palestine, as might have been expected if the Greek language prevailed in that country. To our mind nothing could be plainer than the evidence which the New Testament itself furnishes that the Greek translation of the LXX. *was* so used. This appears from the whole structure of the New Testament, but especially from the manner in which the quotations made by Christ from the Old Testament are preserved. These almost always agree with the Greek translation, even where that differs considerably from the Hebrew; and had not our Saviour actually sanctioned these variations by himself adopting and employing them, we cannot believe that the inspired writers would have put the words into his mouth. No little support to our argument thus accrues from this, as from several other of the objections; but we are willing to let our cause rest on the grounds

[k] It may be observed that Dr. Davidson, while giving the clause *καὶ γλαφυρότητι λέξεων τὸν λόγον ἐπικομψεύοντας* in the Greek, which he quotes from Josephus, entirely omits it in his translation. This has, no doubt, been done from mere inadvertence, but the words should be noticed as having a somewhat important bearing on the meaning to be attached to the whole passage.

which have been already adduced, and content ourselves with a mere refutation of the objection.[1]

Enough, it is believed, has been said above, with respect to the occasional occurrence of Aramaic words and phrases in the New Testament. It has been shown, that nothing could be more natural than that such terms should occur, if the relation of the two languages was such as we suppose. But there is one such term which demands special notice, as it is relied upon not a little by those who uphold the prevalence of Hebrew. We refer to the word *Aceldama*, which occurs in the address of St. Peter (Acts i. 19),—"And it was known unto all the dwellers at Jerusalem; insomuch as that field is called in their proper tongue, Aceldama, that is to say, the Field of Blood." Now, instead of any difficulty, we find in these words new support for our position. Aceldama is composed of two common Aramaic words; and it is vain to imagine, that St. Peter here refers to a *peculiar* Aramaic dialect, as prevailing at Jerusalem, distinct from that of Galilee. Had that been his object, it "would scarcely," as Dr. Alexander remarks, "have been made so prominent, even if his hearers were all Galileans, like himself, which is by no means certain." It was, then, simply to the *Aramaic as such* that he referred, when he spoke of "*their proper* tongue." And this implies, first, that he was at the time speaking in *Greek;* secondly, that Greek, as well as Hebrew, was used in Judæa (else why speak of their *proper* tongue?); and thirdly (from the use of *their* instead of *our*), that Greek, and not Hebrew, was the *common* language of Galilee.

It has also been said, that the preparation of Targums, about the date referred to, in the Aramaic language, proves that that was then the common language of Palestine. But the alleged fact has been much disputed by many eminent scholars, and is of such an uncertain character, that it cannot be admitted as an element in the discussion. Eichhorn and others, contend stoutly,

[1] That the Greek translation *was* used, to some extent at least, in the synagogues of Palestine, see on the Hellenists (Acts vi. 1) Alford's notes. "Hellenists here," says Dr. Alexander, "are *Jews using the Greek language in their worship*." But see as a proof *instar omnium* Luke iv. 18, 19, as compared with the Hebrew.

that the oldest of them—that of Onkelos—does not extend beyond the third century. It is certain that they were entirely unknown to Origen and Jerome,—fathers who were well skilled in the Hebrew language and literature.

The only other objection that we know of, is of an *à priori* character. It rests on the assumed "tenacity of vernacular language;" and the special unlikelihood, in the case of the Jews, that any other tongue should have supplanted their ancient national language. To this kind of argument the best answer is *facts;* and to these, as stated above, we refer. As Dr. Tregelles remarks (and here we have the pleasure of heartily agreeing with him),—"Arguments *à priori* may be very valuable for showing a probability where there is no *evidence*, or where it is doubtful, but the least portion of proved *fact* will destroy all the mere probability." This is a sufficient answer to the objection, since facts *have* been produced to show, that, to a great extent, Hebrew had given way to Greek in Palestine. At the same time, we beg it to be remembered, that on our supposition, Hebrew *continued* in the days of Christ, to be the mother-tongue of all native Jews, and had by no means been utterly "supplanted" by the Greek. Even admitting, then, the force of the *à priori* argument (which, however, is sufficiently flexible to be turned the other way, as Diodati has shown), it is a *telum imbelle*, so far as our position is concerned.

We have proved, then, as is believed, beyond the reach of all reasonable objection, and from the undeniable facts of the New Testament history, that Greek, and not Hebrew, was the common language of religious address in Palestine in the days of Christ and his Apostles. There yet remains one overwhelming argument, as it appears to us, in support of this position, that, viz., which is found in the phenomena presented by the Gospels, *when they are compared with one another*. But this argument naturally runs into the other, for the proper originality of our existing Gospel of St. Matthew, which is to be found in its internal character; and as that point is to engage our attention in the following chapter, it may, in the meantime, be left untouched. But has not the proposition, which we laid down at the commencement of this chapter, been already established? Has not proof sufficient been brought forward, that "the Greek language was widely diffused, well understood, and commonly employed in Palestine, in the time of Christ and his Apostles?" If our readers agree with us, that this has been done, we may, without going further, be allowed to express our gratification at the thought, that, in our existing Greek Gospels, we possess, for the most part, the *very words* of Him to whom the illustrious testimony was borne,—"Never man spake like this man." *He* spoke in Greek, and his Disciples did the same while they reported what He said. Their inspiration consisted not, as some have deemed, in being enabled to give perfect translations, either of discourses delivered, or of documents written, in the Aramaic language, but in being led, under infallible guidance, to transfer to paper for the benefit of all coming ages, those words of the Great Teacher, which they had heard from His lips in the *Greek* tongue; which had, in that form, been imprinted on their affectionate memories; and which were by them in the same language unerringly committed to writing, while they literally experienced a fulfilment of the gracious promise,—"The Comforter, which is the Holy Ghost, whom the Father will send in my name, He shall teach you all things, and bring all things to your remembrance, whatsoever I have said unto you."

# CHAPTER III.

## INTERNAL EVIDENCE OF THE PROPER ORIGINALITY OF THE EXISTING GREEK GOSPEL OF ST. MATTHEW.

### SECTION I.—PROOF FROM A COMPARISON OF THE FIRST THREE GOSPELS.

As every Biblical scholar is aware, there is no question connected with the Gospels, which has been felt more difficult or perplexing, than that which respects their *origin*. So striking are the coincidences, and, at the same time, so strange are the diversities between them, that criticism has been tasked to the uttermost, to give any satisfactory, or even probable, account of the manner in which they may have arisen; and has, by the manifold and mutually destructive theories which it has devised to solve the problem, virtually confessed itself baffled in dealing with this subject.

It is no part of our purpose, and would vastly exceed our limits, to give even the faintest sketch of the various hypotheses which have been suggested in order to meet the difficulties of this question. German ingenuity has wearied itself to no purpose in this department of sacred criticism; and British scholarship has devoted itself, over and over again, to the same fruitless labour. The names of Griesbach, Michaelis, Eichhorn, Gratz, Schleiermacher, and many others among foreign critics, are well known to all Biblical students, in connexion with this question; and those of Bishops Marsh, Gleig, and others, are equally well known at home; while, in our own day, numerous conflicting hypotheses continue to be framed on the Continent, and are, with less or more variation, repeated by Biblical critics in this country.

The most elaborate, and probably, on the whole, most accepted theory which has ever been formed on this subject, is the celebrated one of Eichhorn and Bishop Marsh, which was proposed, in the first instance, by the German scholar, then extended and improved by the English dignitary, and last of all, fully perfected by the labours of its original author. In the various modifications through which it thus passed, before it at length assumed its *ne plus ultra* of perfection, it furnishes an eminent illustration of the difficulties which embarrass this question: and it may here be brought more particularly under the notice of our readers, as a specimen of the toil and ingenuity which have been expended on the subject.

The foundation of the theory is the assumed existence of an Urevangelium, or original Gospel, in the Aramaic language. This original work is supposed to have contained all the sections common to the three Evangelists, but to have been used by them in different forms or editions. Whenever all the three agree, they must have all drawn immediately from the original document: when two of them agree, they must have used a common modified edition of it: and when one has any thing peculiar, he must have derived it from an edition of the original work, which he alone employed, or from some other unknown source. The original writing being supposed in the Aramaic language, Eichhorn imagined that he could thus naturally explain both the differences and agreements of a verbal kind, which are observable among the first three Evangelists. Their differences were accounted for, on the ground of their being independent translators; and their agreements, by their having hit upon many similar modes of expression in translating from a common document. Eichhorn's hypothesis, then, as at first propounded, stood thus:[m]

1. The original Aramaic Gospel.

2. A modified edition of this, which was the foundation of Matthew (A).

3. Another edition, which was the foundation of Luke (B).

4. A third edition, blending A and B, the foundation of Mark (C).

5. A fourth edition, used in common by Matthew and Luke, and explaining their agreement where they differ from Mark (D).

[m] De Wette, Einl. in N. T., § 84, b.

Ingenious as this theory must be admitted to have been, it needed no lengthened consideration of it to discover that it was far from meeting all the requirements of the case. Its manifestly weak point was, that it left unaccounted for, the remarkable agreement which sometimes appears among the Evangelists, even in regard to the use of the rarest and most striking Greek expressions.[n] Thus, both Matthew and Luke employ the words, *πτερύγιον τοῦ ἱεροῦ* (Matt. iv. 5; Luke iv. 9); and *ἐπιούσιος* (Matt. vi. 11; Luke xi. 3); words of such extreme singularity, that the greatest difficulty has been felt, up to the present day, in fixing their exact meaning. Again, all the three Evangelists concur in using the word *δυσκόλως*, in one passage only, and there in the unusual sense of "hardly," or "difficultly," for which the common classical expression was *δυσχερῶς*, or *χαλεπῶς*; whereas *δυσκόλως*, when it occurs in the classics, means "peevishly," or "morosely" (Matt. xix. 23; Mark x. 23; Luke xviii. 24). And it has been observed, that the adverb thus peculiarly made use of by all three Evangelists, is found no where else, either in the New Testament, the Septuagint, or the Greek Apocryphal books.[n] Further, they all employ the striking phrase *οὐ μὴ γεύσονται θανάτου* (Matt. xvi. 22, Mark ix. 1, Luke ix. 27), though they differ from each other in the rest of the sentence in which this expression occurs. And to give only one other example of their striking coincidences; they all agree in the citation, *κατασκευάσει τὴν ὁδόν σου* (Matt. xi. 10, Mark i. 2, Luke vii. 27), and thus concur in differing both from the Septuagint and the Hebrew (Mal. iii. 1). This is a very important case of agreement; for, as our Lord here changes the person from *μου* to *σου*, He makes that which in the Hebrew is said by Jehovah of himself to be spoken to the Messiah; and by thus suggesting his own true Godhead, He furnishes a reason for the variation here made from the original text, and which has been so remarkably preserved by all the three Evangelists.

It was obvious, from a consideration of these and other instances, that the theory of Eichhorn, as to the origin of the Gospels, was not sufficient; and that nothing but the assumption of a common

[n] Marsh's Diss. p. 75, etc.

*Greek* source, in addition to the original Aramaic Gospel which had been conceived of, would account for the striking verbal coincidences exhibited by the Evangelists in their employment of the most remarkable Greek expressions. The want thus felt in the theory of Eichhorn was endeavoured to be supplied by Bishop Marsh, through means of his well-known and elaborate hypothesis. This, as stated by himself, is as follows:—" St. Matthew, St. Mark, St. Luke, all three used copies of the common Hebrew document ℵ, the materials of which St. Matthew, who wrote in Hebrew, retained in the language in which he found them, but St. Mark and St. Luke translated them into Greek. They had no knowledge of each other's Gospel; but St. Mark and St. Luke, besides the copies of the Hebrew document ℵ, used a Greek translation of it, which had been made before any of the additions $\alpha$, $\beta$, etc., had been inserted. Lastly, as the Gospels of St. Mark and St. Luke contained Greek translations of Hebrew materials which were incorporated into St. Matthew's Hebrew Gospel, the person who translated St. Matthew's Hebrew Gospel into Greek frequently derived assistance from the Gospel of St. Mark, where St. Mark had matter in common with St. Matthew; and in those places, but in those places only, where St. Mark had no matter in common with Matthew, he had frequently recourse to St. Luke's Gospel." Such is the famous hypothesis of Bishop Marsh, as set forth by its author: as analysed, and exhibited in the usual form, it is given by De Wette as follows:—

1. The original Aramaic Gospel. ($\aleph$).
2. A translation of it into Greek. ($\overline{\aleph}$).
3. An edition of this work with smaller and larger additions. ($\aleph + \alpha + \text{A}$).
4. Another edition, with other similar additions. ($\aleph + \beta + \text{B}$).
5. An edition, blending both the former, and which became the foundation of Mark. ($\aleph + \alpha + \text{A} + \beta + \text{B}$).
6. An edition, with a greater number of additions like $\alpha + \text{A}$, which formed the foundation of Matthew. ($\aleph + \alpha + \text{A} + \gamma + \Gamma 1$).
7. An edition, with a greater number of additions like $\beta + \text{B}$, and also including the additions $\gamma + \Gamma 1$, which formed the foundation of Luke. ($\aleph + \beta + \text{B} + \gamma + \Gamma 1$).
8. Besides this, Matthew and Luke availed themselves of yet

another original Gospel ב, their common but independent use of which accounts for the passages ($\Gamma$ 2) which they both possess beyond Mark, but which they respectively arrange in a different order.

It was fondly imagined by its author that this intricate hypothesis sufficed to account for all the phenomena of verbal agreement and disagreement presented by the Gospels; but how little he persuaded others to take this favourable view of his labours will be apparent from the following remarks of Dr. Hales, in his "Analysis of Chronology" (vol. iii. p. 8). Having quoted a statement of Bishop Marsh to the effect that "in translating from Hebrew into Greek, there is still less probability of agreeing by *mere accident* than in translating from Greek into English, because the Greek language admits of much greater variety both in the choice and the position of the words than the English language," Hales subjoins, "Thus we are indebted to the learned and ingenious author of this Dissertation for a plain and simple refutation of his own abstruse and complicated hypothesis in all its parts; satisfactory as it should seem to every unprejudiced and unbiassed critic."

But the work of elaboration and improvement was not yet completed. Eichhorn had still to expand to its full dimensions his own original proposal, as now amended and developed by Marsh. Dissatisfied, as it would appear, with the explanations and additions of the English bishop, Eichhorn set himself anew to a further extension of his hypothesis; and adopting from Marsh the idea of a common Greek translation of the original Aramaic Gospel, as absolutely necessary in order to account for the remarkable verbal coincidences of the Evangelists, he at last proposed his scheme for reconciling all difficulties as follows:—

1. The original Aramaic Gospel.

2. A Greek translation of this.

3. A revised edition of the original Gospel employed by Matthew. (A.)

4. A Greek translation of this edition, based upon the Greek translation of the original Gospel.

5. A revised edition of the original Gospel, untranslated into Greek, made use of by Luke. (B.)

6. A mixed edition of A and B, still untranslated into Greek, employed by Mark. (C.)

7. A fourth edition of the original Gospel, employed by Matthew and Luke, in places where they agree with one another, and differ from Mark. (D.)

8. A Greek translation of this fourth edition, influenced by (2) the Greek translation of the original Gospel.

9. The Hebrew Gospel of Matthew arising from a union of A and D. (E.)

10. The Greek translation of Matthew modified by the already existing Greek translation of A and D.

11. A + B (= C) formed the foundation of Mark's Gospel; and Mark, in translating from these sources, used the already existing translation of A; but so far as he used B, had himself to translate it into the Greek language.

12. B + D (= F) gave rise to Luke's Gospel; but, independently of these, there was inserted the account of a journey. In translating into Greek, Luke used the existing translation of D; but, as respected B, had himself to make the translation.

Beyond this, the critical imagination could not be expected to go; and accordingly, no later attempts have been made in the direction followed by Eichhorn and Marsh. But the practice of system-building still continues in other forms, although with equally fruitless results. Either on the ground, (1) That one or two of the Gospels were taken from one another; or, (2) That all three were derived from some common source, either written or traditional, or both; or, (3) That the writers not only used each other's works, but had access, at the same time, to common sources, —critics still labour at the Sisyphian toil of constructing theories, in order to solve this obstinate and perplexing problem.[o] In our own day, De Wette, Hug, Guerike, Norton, Davidson, Alford, Smith of Jordanhill, and many others, have all proposed their several schemes of explanation and agreement; but, as Dr. Tregelles remarks, "The more recent theories on the subject of the harmonizing Gospels, are in general only repetitions of former

[o] For an account of the various theories, see De Wette, Einl. in Das N. T., or Horne's Introduction, vol. iv. 641, etc.

schemes, with or without new modifications." And the problem appears at this moment to remain as far from solution as ever.

In these circumstances, it is with no small diffidence, that we venture to make another contribution to the chaos of opinions that have already been collected on this subject. Our argument, however, in support of the proper originality of the Greek Gospel of St. Matthew, requires us to do so, and does, we believe, point to the much-desired solution. We are firmly convinced, that, as in the Ptolemæan system of the heavens, it was *human speculation* which had introduced difficulty and complexity among God's works, while, in truth, their motions were all regulated with a beautiful simplicity; so here, it is *criticism itself* which has caused the perplexity in connexion with the Divine Word, while, in fact, the phenomena which it presents may all be explained in the easiest and simplest manner. With this conviction, we offer another hypothesis on this much-vexed subject. And in doing so, it is no small satisfaction to reflect, that the theory we are about to state, is distinguished at least by its simplicity; that it needs no algebraic signs in order to make it intelligible; but that it may be set in a single short sentence before our readers, with the assurance that they will all *understand* it, whether or not they may also be induced to *adopt* it.

Our hypothesis, then, is simply this:—*The Lord Jesus Christ* SPOKE IN GREEK, *and the Evangelists independently narrated his actions, and reported his discourses,* IN THE SAME LANGUAGE *which He had Himself employed.*

This theory we propose, as adequate to account for *all* the phenomena presented by the first three Gospels; and thus, as marked out by its sufficiency, no less than by its simplicity, from all those that have preceded it. However ingenious some of these may have appeared, they have neither been simple nor sufficient; and while, from their complexity destitute of all *prima facie* probability, the least practical application which has been made of them, has shown that they could not meet the requirements of the case.

It will be observed, that two perplexing elements which enter into the statement of the problem as most have dealt with it, are at once eliminated from it by the theory which we have proposed. These are, *first*, that our Lord spoke usually in Hebrew, so that our present Greek Gospels must, for the most part, be regarded as containing translations of his words; and, *secondly*, that St. Matthew wrote originally in Hebrew; and that, accordingly, the existing Greek Gospel which bears his name, must be dealt with as a version of his work. The complexity thus introduced into the question is enormous; and we cannot wonder, that with these two ideas assumed as facts, and admitted as elements in the problem to be solved, critics should have been so sorely puzzled by the *data* with which they were furnished, and should scarcely, in any case, have been able to do more than demolish the theories of their predecessors, without, in any measure, succeeding in establishing their own.

The hypothesis which we have proposed, and which we now proceed to illustrate, simple and obvious as it appears, has never, so far as we are aware, been heretofore suggested.[p] This fact increases the hesitation with which we propose it; and leads us to fear that, like many others which have preceded it, it may possess attractions and advantages only in the estimation of its author, while none but he will be blind to its imperfections. But it is with confidence, nevertheless, that we submit it to the candid consideration of all that are interested in this important subject. We have gained no small vantage-ground in the preceding chapter, if we have there succeeded, on other grounds, in making it at least probable, that our Lord did, for the most part, make use of the Greek language; and if now we find, that the theory of the origin of the Gospels which assumes that fact, explains difficulties which cannot otherwise be removed, we may, in that case, not only regard the hypothesis itself as established, but may view it as imparting to our former proposition, all the force and evidence of demonstration.

There are two conditions which must be fulfilled by any theory proposed on this subject, before it can be deemed successful: it must afford a satisfactory explanation, both of the *coincidences* and

[p] Alford refers, in the Prolegomena to his first vol. p. 29, to "A Chapter on the Harmonizing Gospels" by the late Duke of Manchester, in which, perhaps, a similar theory is maintained, but we have not been able to obtain a sight of the work in question.

the *differences* observable in the first three Gospels. It is quite possible to effect the one object, while overlooking or missing the other; but unless *both* are aimed at and attained, the real difficulties of the case have not been faced, and the problem must still be regarded as unsolved.

The coincidences naturally first attract our notice; and by these, therefore, in the first place, we shall endeavour to test and illustrate the value of our hypothesis. As every one knows, these coincidences are very numerous and striking. They are perceptible in every part of the first three Evangelists, so far as the writers deal with the same topics, or cover the same ground. But it is to be observed that they are *most notable by far in reports of what was said, either by the Saviour or others.* And this is a point to which we solicit special attention, as bearing very materially upon the success of our argument. The fact itself has often been remarked, and is indeed generally referred to by writers on the subject; but its great importance in the question now under discussion, warrants and requires that it should here be somewhat more fully considered. Before proceeding, therefore, to the application which we mean to make of it, we shall state it in the words of two eminent critics, and shall bring forward some of the examples in proof of it, to which they refer in the writings of the Evangelists.

"All the three," says Credner, "frequently agree in their expressions, and that in such a manner that sections which, at the beginning, manifest much divergence, become more and more alike as they approach the principal topic; while, in regard to this leading subject, they exhibit a *verbal identity, particularly in the words of Jesus*, and most of all in prophecies or maxims, and then begin again to diverge more or less from one another."[q] In illustration of what is here stated, we may quote the following passages:—

[q] Credner, Einl. § 67, 1.

### MATTHEW viii. 2, 3.

Καὶ ἰδοὺ, λεπρὸς ἐλθὼν προσεκύνει αὐτῷ λέγων· Κύριε, ἐὰν θέλῃς, δύνασαί με καθαρίσαι. Καὶ ἐκτείνας τὴν χεῖρα, ἥψατο αὐτοῦ ὁ Ἰησοῦς, λέγων· Θέλω, καθαρίσθητι. Καὶ εὐθέως ἐκαθαρίσθη αὐτοῦ ἡ λέπρα.

### MARK i. 40–42.

Καὶ ἔρχεται πρὸς αὐτὸν λεπρὸς, παρακαλῶν αὐτὸν καὶ γονυπετῶν αὐτὸν, καὶ λέγων αὐτῷ· Ὅτι, ἐὰν θέλῃς, δύνασαί με καθαρίσαι. Ὁ δὲ Ἰησοῦς σπλαγχνισθεὶς, ἐκτείνας τὴν χεῖρα, ἥψατο αὐτοῦ, καὶ λέγει αὐτῷ· Θέλω, καθαρίσθητι. Καὶ εἰπόντος αὐτοῦ, εὐθέως ἀπῆλθεν ἀπ' αὐτοῦ ἡ λέπρα, καὶ ἐκαθαρίσθη·

### LUKE v. 12, 13.

Καὶ ἐγένετο ἐν τῷ εἶναι αὐτὸν ἐν μιᾷ τῶν πόλεων, καὶ ἰδοὺ, ἀνὴρ πλήρης λέπρας· καὶ ἰδὼν τὸν Ἰησοῦν, πεσὼν ἐπὶ πρόσωπον, ἐδεήθη αὐτοῦ, λέγων· Κύριε, ἐὰν θέλῃς, δύνασαί με καθαρίσαι. Καὶ ἐκτείνας τὴν χεῖρα, ἥψατο αὐτοῦ, εἰπών· Θέλω, καθαρίσθητι. Καὶ εὐθέως ἡ λέπρα ἀπῆλθεν ἀπ' αὐτοῦ.

### MATTHEW ix. 5, 6.

Τί γάρ ἐστιν εὐκοπώτερον, εἰπεῖν, Ἀφέωνταί σου αἱ ἁμαρτίαι· ἢ εἰπεῖν, Ἔγειρε καὶ περιπάτει; ἵνα δὲ εἰδῆτε, ὅτι ἐξουσίαν ἔχει ὁ υἱὸς τοῦ ἀνθρώπου ἐπὶ τῆς γῆς ἀφιέναι ἁμαρτίας, (τότε λέγει τῷ παραλυτικῷ·) Ἐγερθεὶς ἆρόν σου τὴν κλίνην, καὶ ὕπαγε εἰς τὸν οἶκόν σου.

### MARK ii. 9–11.

Τί ἐστιν εὐκοπώτερον, εἰπεῖν τῷ παραλυτικῷ· Ἀφέωνταί σου αἱ ἁμαρτίαι· ἢ εἰπεῖν· Ἔγειρε, ἆρόν σου τὸν κράββατον, καὶ περιπάτει; ἵνα δὲ εἰδῆτε, ὅτι ἐξουσίαν ἔχει ὁ υἱὸς τοῦ ἀνθρώπου ἐπὶ τῆς γῆς ἀφιέναι ἁμαρτίας· (λέγει τῷ παραλυτικῷ). Σοὶ λέγω· Ἔγειρε, ἆρον τὸν κράββατόν σου, καὶ ὕπαγε εἰς τὸν οἶκόν σου.

### LUKE v. 23, 24.

Τί ἐστιν εὐκοπώτερον, εἰπεῖν· Ἀφέωνταί σοι αἱ ἁμαρτίαι σου, ἢ εἰπεῖν· Ἔγειρε καὶ περιπάτει; ἵνα δὲ εἰδῆτε ὅτι ἐξουσίαν ἔχει ὁ υἱὸς τοῦ ἀνθρώπου ἐπὶ τῆς γῆς ἀφιέναι ἁμαρτίας, (εἶπε τῷ παραλελυμένῳ·) Σοὶ λέγω· Ἔγειρε, καὶ ἄρας τὸ κλινίδιόν σου, πορεύου εἰς τὸν οἶκόν σου.

### MATTHEW xix. 23, 24.

Ὁ δὲ Ἰησοῦς εἶπε τοῖς μαθηταῖς αὐτοῦ· Ἀμὴν λέγω ὑμῖν, ὅτι δυσκόλως πλούσιος εἰσελεύσεται εἰς τὴν βασιλείαν τῶν οὐρανῶν. πάλιν δὲ λέγω ὑμῖν, εὐκοπώτερόν ἐστι κάμηλον διὰ τρυπήματος ῥαφίδος εἰσελθεῖν, ἢ πλούσιον εἰς τὴν βασιλείαν τοῦ Θεοῦ εἰσελθεῖν.

### MARK x. 23–25.

Καὶ περιβλεψάμενος ὁ Ἰησοῦς λέγει τοῖς μαθηταῖς αὐτοῦ· Πῶς δυσκόλως οἱ τὰ χρήματα ἔχοντες εἰς τὴν βασιλείαν τοῦ Θεοῦ εἰσελεύσονται. Οἱ δὲ μαθηταὶ ἐθαμβοῦντο ἐπὶ τοῖς λόγοις αὐτοῦ. ὁ δὲ Ἰησοῦς πάλιν ἀποκριθεὶς λέγει αὐτοῖς· Τέκνα, πῶς δύσκολόν ἐστι τοὺς πεποιθότας ἐπὶ τοῖς χρήμασιν εἰς τὴν βασιλείαν τοῦ Θεοῦ εἰσελθεῖν. εὐκοπώτερόν ἐστι κάμηλον διὰ τῆς τρυμαλιᾶς τῆς ῥαφίδος διελθεῖν, ἢ πλούσιον εἰς τὴν βασιλείαν τοῦ Θεοῦ εἰσελθεῖν.

### LUKE xviii. 24, 25.

Ἰδὼν δὲ αὐτὸν ὁ Ἰησοῦς περίλυπον γενόμενον εἶπε· Πῶς δυσκόλως οἱ τὰ χρήματα ἔχοντες εἰσελεύσονται εἰς τὴν βασιλείαν τοῦ Θεοῦ. εὐκοπώτερον γάρ ἐστι, κάμηλον διὰ τρυμαλιᾶς ῥαφίδος εἰσελθεῖν, ἢ πλούσιον εἰς τὴν βασιλείαν τοῦ Θεοῦ εἰσελθεῖν.

Many similar examples might be quoted; but the above, taken almost at random, are sufficient for our present purpose. The striking verbal coincidences which they exhibit as existing between the three Evangelists are at once apparent; and it will be noticed, as Credner states, that these are by far most marked and exact in reports of our Lord's words, or of the words of others. It will also be observed, as in the first example, that, with considerable variation both before and afterwards, the address of the leprous man to Christ, and our Lord's reply to him, are given in exactly the same words by all three Evangelists.

Let us now quote a passage from an American critic, who has devoted a great deal of attention to this subject; and we shall find that he brings out exactly the same thing, accompanied, however, by some further valuable remarks. In his work on "The Genuineness of the Gospels" (vol. i. 240), Professor Norton writes as follows:—

"The occurrence of passages verbally the same, or strikingly coincident in the use of many of the same words, which appearances I shall denote by the term *verbal coincidence*, or *verbal agreement*, particularly demands attention. . . . . By far the larger portion of this verbal agreement is found in the recital of *the words* of others, and particularly of *the words* of Jesus. Thus, in Matthew's Gospel, the passages verbally coincident with one or both of the other two Gospels, amount to less than a sixth part of its contents; and of this, about *seven-eighths* occur in the recital of the words of others, and only about *one-eighth* in what, by way of distinction, I may call mere narrative, in which the Evangelist, speaking in his own person, was unrestrained in the choice of his expressions. In Mark, the proportion of coincident passages to the whole contents of the Gospel, is only about one-sixth, of which not *one-fifth* occurs in the narrative. Luke has still less agreement of expression with the other Evangelists. The proportion in which it is found amounts only to about a tenth part of his Gospel, and but an inconsiderable portion of it appears in the narrative; in which there are very few instances of its existence for more than half-a-dozen words together. In the narrative, it may be computed as less than a *twentieth* part.

"These definite proportions are important, as showing distinctly in how small a part of each Gospel there is any verbal coincidence with either of the other two; and to how great a degree such coincidence is confined to passages in which the evangelists professedly *give the words of others*, particularly of Jesus."

Such then is the state of matters in regard to the verbal coincidences existing in the first three Gospels: they are by far most numerous and most striking in those passages which report the words of others, and particularly the words of Christ himself; let us now apply our hypothesis to the explanation of these facts, and see whether or not it will prove sufficient.

Jesus, we believe, spoke in Greek, and the Evangelists professedly report his words in the same language. Would we not expect then in such a case that there should be striking verbal coincidences among them? It is plain that it could not be otherwise, provided they were duly qualified for the task which they had undertaken. Here are three writers all professing to give us a report of what the Saviour uttered, and all, as we conceive, writing in the language which He employed—it follows then of course, that if they were well-informed they must often strikingly agree in what they relate. The only thing that could hinder verbal coincidences, would be a defect in the fulness or correctness of their information: and the existence of such coincidences (supposing them independent writers) is the most complete and decisive proof of their accurate knowledge, which could be conceived. It would, of course, be in reports of what was *said* by our Lord and others, that they would be most of all expected to agree; there might and would necessarily be differences in the narrative portions, though in it also, from various causes, we would naturally expect occasional agreement. Two or more reporters in our own day, giving an account of a public meeting, would of necessity agree chiefly and verbally in their statements of what was *said;* in their descriptions of the scene, the order of events, and the effects produced on the individuals present, they would as naturally differ to a considerable extent, yet also probably to some extent verbally agree. And thus it is with our Evangelists. The far larger proportion of their coincidences is to be found in what they *report;* a small portion only in what they *narrate.* And this is exactly what we would expect from those who were competent to give us a history of our Saviour. That the writers of our Gospels were thus competent, appears not only from their works, but from what we know of themselves. Matthew as an apostle was himself a witness of the things which he related: Mark, as is almost universally admitted, wrote under the eye of the apostle Peter, who also was one of those who were present "all the time that the Lord Jesus went in and out" among his disciples; and Luke, as he expressly tells us, "had accurately traced out all the facts of the Evangelic history from the beginning," and thus, if not himself an eye or ear-witness, had taken care to obtain his information from such as were so, and then carefully to arrange it in the narrative which he composed.

Thus then, on our supposition that the Lord Jesus Christ *spoke* in Greek, and that St. Matthew, St. Mark and St. Luke *all wrote* in Greek, there is no difficulty whatever in accounting for the verbal agreement in our first three Gospels: the difficulty would have arisen had the fact been otherwise. If the Evangelists were qualified to write a history of Christ at all, and to give us an account of his discourses; still more, if, as we believe, they wrote under the influence of the Holy Spirit of promise, who guided their thoughts and strengthened their memories, while at the same time their own minds were allowed full play, and their own special endowments and acquirements employed—if these things were so, it could not have been otherwise, than that they should frequently concur in the use of words and phrases, and all the more so, if these happened, as originally spoken, to be of a striking or unusual character.[r]

[r] The only difficulty which we can imagine any one still to feel in connexion with our hypothesis, is how to account for those verbal coincidences which occur in the properly *narrative* portion of the three Evangelists. These coincidences, as stated in the text, are comparatively few, and do not generally extend beyond a few words. The "most remarkable example" of this kind of harmony, is the following in Mat. xiv. 19; Mark vi. 41; and Luke ix. 16; in all which passages we find the words, *λαβὼν τοὺς πέντε ἄρτους, καὶ τοὺς δύο ἰχθύας, ἀναβλέψας εἰς τὸν οὐρανὸν εὐλόγησε.* When it is considered that this is really the only case in which the three Evangelists coincide for more than a few words in the narrative part of the Gospels, we do not think that any reader will be inclined to attach much importance to the difficulty which we have thought it right to notice. But, even if such coincidences had been far more numerous and striking than they are, there is an explanation which

But, introduce now the idea of Christ having spoken in one language, and the Evangelists having written in another; or, what amounts to the same thing, of our present Gospel of St. Matthew being a translation instead of an original work, and instant and insuperable difficulty arises. The question then is, how to account for the (in that case) truly marvellous coincidences of words and phrases which occur in the first three Gospels. These cannot be attributed either to accident or inspiration. Accident, as every one knows, scarcely ever leads to identity of expression among different writers. They may often concur in the thoughts, but rarely indeed in the form which their thoughts assume. "It has been noted," says a recent writer in the *Athenæum*, "that Terence says, 'I præ, sequar,' and that some modern dramatists have hit on, 'Go before, I'll follow.' This is, perhaps, nearly the utmost extent to which different writers fall on the same collocations of words: from five or six at a time." And while accident will not explain the striking verbal agreements in our first three Gospels, it is still worse to seek any aid in this matter from inspiration. Inspiration will never account for needless miracles. And here, if there was no natural foundation in the actual circumstances of the writers for the coincidences which appear among them, the miracles must have been as countless as they were

can be given that appears completely to remove any difficulty which may thus be felt. We shall state it in the words of Prof. Norton (i. 288): "the twelve Apostles, who were companions of our Saviour, *resided together* at Jerusalem, we know not for how long a period, certainly for several years; acting and preaching in concert. This being the case, they would confer together continually: they would be present at each other's discourses, in which the events of their Master's life were related: they would in common give instruction respecting his history and doctrine to new converts, especially to those who were to go forth as missionaries. From all these circumstances, their modes of narrating the same events would become assimilated to each other." This consideration completely relieves our hypothesis of every difficulty, however little it may help Prof. Norton himself, who both supposes that the Apostles often spoke in *Aramaic*, and that Matthew's Gospel was originally written in that language. On *our* supposition that they almost always *spoke in Greek*, and that St. Matthew, like the other Evangelists, *wrote* in the same language, there is no difficulty in supposing that certain forms of expression became stereotyped, so to speak, in the narrative so frequently repeated by the Apostles, and were thus naturally adopted in common by the writers of our first three Gospels.

unnecessary. Enough then of these first two causes; and there remain only two other suppositions possible, if the hypothesis which we have proposed be not accepted. These are, either the Urevangelium, or original-gospel theory of Eichhorn and Marsh, or, if that be rejected, the hypothesis that the Evangelists *copied* from one another.

And this latter accordingly is the expedient which in one form or another the maintainers of the Hebrew original of Matthew's Gospel, who reject the former theory, are compelled to adopt. Thus says Mill (Proleg. in N. T. 109), "Factâ collatione singulorum utriusque evangelii, quæ quidem idem argumentum tractant, capitum, *inevitabili plane necessitate coactus sum* ut credam ne quidem aliter fieri potuisse, quin Marcus qui cum Matthæo in plurimis exacte, ac veluti ad verbum, convenit, *Matthæi evangelium habuerit ad manum* cum suum appareret." Again, he says with respect to the Gospel of St. Luke, (§ 116) "Certe evulgatum fuisse illud, post editionem evangeliorum Matt. et Mar. ex collatione trium horum inter se luce clarius apparet. Nihil scilicet evidentius quam D. Lucam evangelium Matt. et Mar. ipsas ῥήσεις phrases—ac locutiones imo—vero totas periochas *in suum* nonnunquam *αὐτολεξεὶ traduxisse.*" Examples are then brought forward.

It is perfectly certain then, by their own confession, that the defenders of the Hebrew original of St. Matthew, are compelled, in order to give any account of the numerous verbal coincidences between our present Greek Gospels, either to rest in some such hypothesis as that of Eichhorn, or to suppose that the Evangelists copied from each other. "It seems to me," says Cureton, (Syriac Gospels, p. xc.) "that no candid person who is sufficiently acquainted with the language and the subject, after having fully entered into the examination, can fail to acquiesce in the conclusion arrived at by Bishop Marsh, that '*The table of parallel and coincident passages*,' as shewn in his Dissertation, '*is one continued proof, either that the Hebrew text of St. Matthew was the basis of the Gospels of St. Mark and St. Luke, or that some common document*,' that is, Hebrew or Aramaic, '*was the basis of all three Gospels.*'"

We leave it to the advocates of the Hebrew original of St.

Matthew, to make choice between these two alternatives; but *one or other of them*, according to the declaration of one of themselves, every "candid person" among them *must adopt*, in order to give any explanation of the coincidences which have been mentioned. If they make choice of the original-gospel theory, there is not a single word required, in order to shew the untenableness of their position. The mere illustrations of that theory which were given at the beginning of this chapter, must be quite sufficient to overthrow it. Indeed, so palpable are its improbabilities, and so evident its defects, that, as De Wette remarks,[s] one can only wonder how it should have formerly met with so much approbation.

If, on the other hand, they choose to maintain that the Evangelists copied from one another, and in this way account for the coincidences which appear between them, the question instantly occurs, how the *differences* which are equally striking, are then to be explained. As before remarked, every sufficient hypothesis must furnish a satisfactory account both of the *differences* and the *coincidences;* and if it fails with regard to one of these, it fails entirely. Whatever theory then is proposed upon this subject, must be tested by the diversities apparent in the first three Gospels as well as by their agreements, and although sufficient to account for the one class of phenomena, must still be pronounced wanting in an essential requisite to completeness, if it offers no satisfactory explanation of the other.

It has already been proved, that the hypothesis which we have proposed, fully accounts for the coincidences; and now, a very few words will be sufficient to show, that it also affords a full explanation of the divergencies. We suppose that the three Evangelists were all well-informed on the subject on which they wrote, and were all under the guidance of the Holy Spirit in composing their works, but that, at the same time, they were independent writers, of different talents, habits and tendencies, and to a certain extent having a different purpose in view by the publication of their Gospels. It follows, of course, that in such a case, while there will be much agreement, there must also be

[s] "Dass man sich jetzt fast nur wundern knan, wie diese Hypothese früherhin so vielen Beifall finden konnte." (Einl. § 85.)

no small diversity, and that the narrative portion especially, will be marked by many little variations, since in that part the writer was free to manifest his own special character and attainments. And thus, as we need scarcely remark, the case really stands. Let our readers look back to the second example quoted in illustration of the coincidences, and they will observe many striking little diversities. Mark appears as usual the most diffuse and particular; Matthew and Luke with a very close general agreement, yet vary in several of their expressions, while all the Evangelists differ, as Norton has remarked, in the terms they use respectively for "bed," Matthew having *κλίνη*, Mark *κράββατος*, and Luke *κλινίδιον*. Our theory leaves full scope for such diversities, and leads us indeed to expect them; so that not only does it fulfil the one condition of accounting for the coincidences, but equally satisfies the other of explaining the differences, and thus is found in every application of it entirely sufficient.[t]

But what shall be said of these divergencies on the theory that the Evangelists made use of each other's works—a theory to which by their own confession the advocates of a Hebrew original are compelled to have recourse? It has been clearly shewn by Prof. Norton (i. 251-263) that no satisfactory account *can* be given of the differences in the Gospels, if it be supposed that the writers copied from one another. "There is," he says, "no reasonable principle of selection on which they can be supposed to have proceeded. They were all of them as preachers of Christianity, well acquainted with the transactions which it was their

[t] It may here be observed that, in all probability, our Lord employed Aramaic on some other occasions than those specially mentioned by the Evangelists. We have no direct and certain evidence that He did so: but I think there is some ground for the supposition, not only in the nature of the case, but in the fact that the Evangelists occasionally vary a little in those accounts which they profess to give us of *short and striking sentences* which He uttered. It appears not improbable that this variation is in some cases to be explained by the supposition that the Saviour then spoke in Aramaic, and that the Evangelists gave us independent translations of his words. We find an illustration of the manner in which verbal differences would thus arise, in the different Greek terms by which St. Mark and St. Luke respectively render the Aramaic words "*talitha cumi*," addressed to Jairus' daughter. The former has *τὸ κοράσιον ἔγειραι*, the latter *ἡ παῖς ἐγείρου*: St. Matthew contains no statement of the words which were employed.

purpose to record: their independent knowledge of them appears in the Gospel of each; they had therefore, no occasion to copy one from another, and it is a fact, obvious simply upon inspection, that far the greater part of each Gospel was not thus copied. And lastly, their Gospels generally, and even those very passages on which this theory of transcription has been founded, present numerous diversities of such a character, as the Evangelist, whichever[u] may be supposed the copyist, would not have made, with the text of his predecessor, or predecessors, before him as an archetype." This writer, however, upholding as he does the Hebrew original of St. Matthew's Gospel, is himself driven at last to adopt the copying theory to some extent. "We *cannot account*," he says (p. 298), "for the remarkable coincidence of language between our Greek translation of Matthew and the other Gospels, but by the supposition, that the translator, through his familiarity with them, was led to adopt their expressions when suitable to his purpose." The same admission and supposition are made by Dr. Davidson in his Introduction to the New Testament (vol. i., 411, etc.) After following much the same course of argument as Prof. Norton with regard to the hypothesis, that one of the Evangelists copied from another, and after endeavouring, also in much the same way, to shew how the coincidences may possibly be explained on other grounds, he at last candidly admits, that all the considerations which he has brought forward, "*are not sufficient of themselves to account for the remarkable coincidences.*" He therefore is compelled, as we have seen is the case also with Norton, to try to eke out his argument by the additional supposition that "the Greek translator of Matthew used the Gospels of

[u] As Alford remarks (Proleg. vol. i. 3), "Different hypotheses of the mutual interdependence of the three have been made, *embracing every possible permutation of their order.*" He subjoins the following illustration of this statement:—

1. That Matthew wrote first—that Mark used his Gospel, and then Luke both these, is held by Grotius, Mill, Wetstein, Townson, Hug, Greswell, etc.
2. Matthew, Luke, Mark,—Griesbach, Fritzsche, Meyer, De Wette, etc.
3. Mark, Matthew, Luke,—Storr and Smith of Jordanhill.
4. Mark, Luke, Matthew,—Weisse, Wilke, Hitzig, etc.
5. Luke, Matthew, Mark,—Büsching and Evanson.
6. Luke, Mark, Matthew,—Vögel.

Mark and Luke, where the matter in the Aramæan was so like the matter of the two Evangelists, as to warrant its being rendered into corresponding or coincident language." All this just serves still more clearly to illustrate the difficulties, in which the defenders of the Hebrew original of Matthew, and of the opinion that our Lord usually spoke in Aramaic, are placed. Some of them must conjure up a phantom-gospel, which they call a Urevangelium, and of which no traces whatever are found in antiquity (Eichhorn, Marsh, etc.,); others of them plainly state that the coincidences are in their view inexplicable unless the two later writers saw and made use of the work of the first (Mill, Greswell, etc.); while others again, admit, though much opposed to the copying theory in general, that they cannot dispense with it in the ease of the translator of Matthew's Hebrew Gospel (Norton, Davidson, etc.).

It is not our purpose so much to expose the weakness of former theories, as, if possible, to establish our own. We would fain be *constructive*, which is ever something higher and better than simply being *destructive:* and there has on the present subject been only too much of the latter, while a lamentable want has been felt of the former. We deem it needless therefore, to dwell at any length on the peculiar schemes of Norton and Davidson, which repudiate the copying hypothesis so far as Mark and Luke are concerned, but hold to it with respect to our existing Matthew. We believe that if it be maintained, as these writers do maintain, that our Lord spoke in Aramaic, no possible explanation can be given of the wonderful coincidences which exist between even *two* of the Evangelists. If Christ spoke in Aramaic, the same cause which led *Him* to do so, must have induced the *Apostles* while they remained in Jerusalem, to a great extent to continue the practice; and thus there would be no scope for the production of that gradually stereotyped form of translation into Greek, by which it is sought to explain the striking phenomena of agreement. Indeed, one of the constant arguments employed by the defenders of the Hebrew original of St. Matthew's Gospel is, that the speech of Paul to the multitude in that language (Acts xxii.), proves that *Hebrew* was the most suitable language in which to address them, and the language therefore which Matthew would naturally adopt in writing to his countrymen. Now, the same argument proves that the Apostles, while still in Jerusalem, would generally *have spoken in Hebrew*, and thus, as has been said, a common Greek form of expression could not have arisen.

Independently of this, however, the theory of Norton and Davidson is, after all, liable to the worst objections which have been brought against the copying hypothesis, as it is usually proposed. These have been stated very forcibly by Alford, (vol. i. Proleg. § ii.) who concludes his remarks as follows:—"I do not see how *any* theory of mutual interdependence will leave to our three Evangelists their credit as *able* or *trustworthy writers*, or even as *honest men;* nor can I find any such theory borne out by the nature of the variations apparent in the respective texts." In this expression of opinion we thoroughly concur; and although Mr. Alford does not specially apply his remarks to such a modification of the copying hypothesis as that maintained by Davidson and Norton, yet that they do so apply, will, we think, be evident from carefully weighing the following considerations.

The supposed translator of St. Matthew must, of course, have had the same *general* object in view as the writer of an original Gospel, viz., the further instruction and edification of professing Christians. He must have felt himself urged to the work by a desire to add to the existing sources of knowledge already open to all who wished to inquire into the history and character of Jesus Christ. He must have wished to convey to the world, in a language generally understood, the *peculiar* statements of St. Matthew on this great subject. Now, how utterly inconsistent with such a purpose was it, that the translator should have helped himself so freely from Gospels already current in the church! To say nothing of the morality of such a proceeding, (a professed translator foisting into his work passages which his author had never *written*, and which he himself had never *translated*, a double deceit!) its folly must at once be apparent. If it was not *St. Matthew's work* which he presented to the world, there was really no object to be served by his labours. St. Mark and St. Luke were already well known, and if he were to help himself so liberally out of their works, as he *has* done, if the copying theory be true, then it is evident that he was not fulfilling the only purpose to be accomplished by his issuing a new Gospel at all. We gratefully acknowledge indeed, that there is much in St. Matthew which we do not find in the other Evangelists, but, on the supposition that it is a translation there should have been more. The translator might have given us in numberless cases the special turns of thought or expression employed by his Author, and in undertaking a version of the Apostle's work, he virtually pledged himself to do so; but instead of that, he has (on the supposition we are combating), pilfered most unscrupulously from already existing narratives, and thus defeated, to a great extent, the object which he had in issuing a translation at all!

What then are the maintainers of the Hebrew original of St. Matthew's Gospel to do? To what side can they turn, and how will they find a means of escape from the difficulties which embarrass them? On the one hand, there is presented to their acceptance the Ur-evangelium hypothesis, with all its "cycles and epicycles" of confusion and perplexity. On the other hand, the theory of mutual interdependence offers its aid, but only to entail difficulties, and to lead to consequences from which every honest heart, and every reflecting mind instinctively shrink. What then are they to do? how explain or defend their position? The most *prudent* course no doubt is to evade the question—to *assert* simply, on the ground of *other assertions*, which are deemed impregnable, that St. Matthew's Gospel, as we now have it, *is a translation*, and to look not at the contradictions and absurdities which on that supposition immediately arise. This is the course followed by Dr. Tregelles. He scarcely *alludes* to the difficulties which his hypothesis engenders. The following, so far as we know, are the only sentences which he has ever penned upon the subject; and let our readers observe how quietly he shelves the annoying questions which, like others, he was bound to face. "The general opinion," he tells us,[v] "of competent critics is that many of the actions and discourses of our Lord were early in oral circulation in a somewhat definite form; and that *this is sufficient to account for the verbal coincidences which we find.*" Who those competent critics are to whom he here refers, we are at a loss to imagine. He names indeed Norton and Davidson, as

[v] Horne and Tregelles, p. 664-5.

if these were the critics intended, but *both* these, as we have seen, expressly admit that the cause which Dr. Tregelles mentions is *not sufficient* to account for the coincidences. They both feel it necessary to conceive that St. Matthew's translation was copied from the other Gospels: whether or not Dr. Tregelles follows them in this, does not appear; but if not, it would be satisfactory to know how he escapes from the necessity which has been felt and acknowledged by those "competent critics" on his own side of the question.

Again he observes, that "it must also be remarked, that elaborate theories quite leave out of sight the plenary inspiration of the Evangelists: if *this* be remembered, it is difficult to suppose that these narratives could have originated from any mechanical accretion of materials; and if *this* be fully admitted, we may, while *owning that verbal coincidences arose from the form that narratives had previously assumed*, see that there was a *definite reason* why the different inspired writers *varied in what they inserted*, and in the manner in which it was connected. The four Gospels have respectively a varying scope, aspect and phase of instruction."

In this passage, there comes out one of the most admirable features in the character of this eminent critic,—his deep respect for the word of God. It is delightful to find among us, *one* at least who, while quite abreast of the most accomplished rationalist as regards scholarship, yet so constantly and emphatically expresses his reverence for Scripture as divinely-inspired truth. But, although rejoicing to agree with Dr. Tregelles in the spirit evinced in the above extract, we cannot at the same time fail to perceive how clearly it reveals the weakness of his position on the present question. He takes for granted that the "verbal coincidences" of the Gospels "arose from the form which narratives had previously assumed;" a supposition which, as we have shewn, is utterly inadequate to account for these coincidences, and the inadequacy of which is *admitted* by the most strenuous supporters of the Hebrew original of St. Matthew. He also supposes, that "the varying scope, aspect and phase of instruction," presented by the several Gospels, furnish a definite reason for their varieties of phrase and arrangement. It is needless to remark on this, that there are numberless divergencies in our first three Gospels, which cannot be accounted for on these grounds, changes of words and clauses which have *no bearing whatever* on the respective "scope, aspect and phase of instruction" of the three Evangelists.

It is vain, moreover, to seek some assistance from the *inspiration* of the writers, as Dr. Tregelles seems inclined to do, in dealing with this subject. Inspiration must never be had recourse to, in order to escape from the difficulties which arise from mere human opinions. If man ties a knot so tangled that he cannot again unloose it, it is little short of impiety to call in divine aid in order to cut it. He must extricate himself from the difficulty in which he has become self-involved; and if that be found impossible, he must confess the error which he has committed. The advocates of the Hebrew original of St. Matthew, are bound to face all the embarrassments which gather round their position. They must give some satisfactory account of the phenomena presented by our existing Gospels. These phenomena are plain and tangible realities; and while there *may be* error in the statements of some ancient fathers on this, as on other subjects, there *can be* no mistake as to the facts which are presented at this day by the Gospels to our own eyes. If then, as we think has been proved, these facts cannot be explained on the hypothesis, either that our Lord spoke for the most part in Hebrew, or that our present Greek Gospel of St. Matthew is a version of a Hebrew original, we must discard both such notions as errors, whoever may sanction or maintain them; and we must cling to that one simple and satisfactory hypothesis, by which, as has been shewn, the whole facts of the case are easily explained, and by which *alone* they become intelligible.

## SECTION II.—PROOFS OF ORIGINALITY FROM THE SPECIAL STRUCTURE OF THE GOSPEL.

We now proceed to a more particular examination of the existing Greek Gospel of St. Matthew, viewed by itself, and shall endeavour to collect the additional probabilities thus furnished in favour of its proper originality. Some such are, of course, to be expected, if the conclusion which we have already reached be in accordance with truth. If St. Matthew, like the other Evangelists, wrote originally in Greek, it is to be supposed that *his* work, no less than theirs, will bear in itself the proper stamp and evidence of originality. And that not a few confirmatory proofs of this kind may be derived from an inspection of the Gospel by itself, we are firmly convinced, and shall endeavour to show. But in entering on this department of the argument, we wish it to be borne in mind, that we do not, in any essential respect, rest our case upon the facts now to be noticed. The *great* proof has already been produced; and if that can be set aside, or if it fail to convince, we are willing to acknowledge, that nothing else which remains to be stated is likely to be successful, and at once to abandon the argument.

But, as we deem it scarcely possible for any impartial investigator, to resist the evidence already adduced in support of the true originality of our present Greek Gospel, it is with the happy feeling of one whose position may *receive*, but does not *require*, additional support, that we proceed to the special object of this section. All the points about to be noticed, appear to us to harmonize most exactly with the result already obtained, and thus more decisively, if that be possible, to evince its accuracy: but we are, at the same time, perfectly aware that some of them will easily admit of cavil or dispute. It will be vain, however, for any one to quarrel with the views which are now to be propounded, unless he has succeeded, first of all, in overturning what has already been established. We are quite willing to rest the whole cause of the proper originality of our existing Gospel of St. Matthew, on the argument, as developed and applied, in the preceding section. That is the ground on which we specially challenge the defenders of the Hebrew original to meet us, and where we desire that the conflict should be decided. But, at the same time, even supposing them successful in setting aside what we deem the fatal objections to their hypothesis, which arise from a comparison of the Gospel of St. Matthew with those of St. Mark and St. Luke, there are still very formidable objections which rise up against them from the Gospel of St. Matthew, viewed by itself. Attempts, it is true, have been made to answer these, and even at times to retort them upon the defenders of the Greek original. But we are firmly convinced, and trust to render apparent, that it is only by an exercise of perverse ingenuity, that this can be effected. All the points now to be touched upon, do, we believe, bear a most friendly aspect towards that view of the question which it is our purpose to defend; and, when allowed to produce their proper impression, harmoniously combine in illustrating and establishing its truthfulness.

In entering, then, on this portion of the argument, we may remark,—

(1.) That on a complete and thorough examination of the Greek Gospel of St. Matthew, *it is seen every where to possess the air and character of an original, and not a translated work.*

The maintainers of the Hebrew original, for the most part, allow that this is the case. Dr. Tregelles makes the admission as fully as can be desired, and simply denies, that on this *one* account it is necessary to abandon the idea of a Hebrew original. "It is granted," he says, "that St. Matthew's Gospel in Greek does not seem like a translation: that the language does not seem less original than the other New Testament writings: and that, unless we had external testimony, we should probably not have imagined it to be a version: but all this does not *prove* the contrary." We are not inclined to press this point with him, and we do not require to do so. There are other grounds, as we have shown, on which we place more dependance in this controversy; but it is something, at least, to get such an explicit admission from one of the most strenuous upholders of the Hebrew original. It will serve as a reply to very different allegations which have been made by some others on the same side of the question. Eichhorn, Davidson, and Cureton, all imagine that there are manifest marks of the translator to be discovered in our existing Greek Gospel. Eichhorn reckons up a vast number of palpable errors, as he deems them,—undertakes, indeed, to show that there are some such to be found in every chapter. Davidson, on the other hand, will not allow that there are any positive mistakes (except, perhaps, in the translation νῖκος, in xii. 20), but traces the hand of the translator in several passages: while Cureton, again, decidedly prefers, in very many cases, the readings of that Syriac recension of St. Matthew, which he recently edited, to our existing Greek, and openly charges the supposed translator with numerous and evident errors.

We shall review the arguments of Cureton at some length in the following chapter, and may, therefore, in the meantime leave them unnoticed. As to the position assumed by Eichhorn, it would be a waste of time to expose its absurdity. All critics are now agreed, that he himself, and not the writer or translator of the Gospel, was the person in error. It is enough to say, in the words of Credner, that "the pretended instances of mistranslation, which Bolten, Eichhorn, and Bertholdt reckon up, have no existence save in their own imagination;"[w] or in those of Dr. Davidson himself, that "those who impugn the authority of the Greek Gospel, desert antiquity, in denying its identity with the Aramæan, written by Matthew, while they maintain the opinion of that same antiquity, concerning the fact of Matthew writing in Hebrew."[x]

We have, then, to concern ourselves, in this place, only with those writers who admit that there are few, or no traces of translation, in our present Gospel of St. Matthew, and yet deem that an unimportant circumstance in connexion with the subject under discussion. They confess that it does not look *like* a translation, but they are not the less inclined, on that account, to conclude that it *is* a translation. It seems to them quite a natural thing that it should appear what it is not,—should bear the character of an original, while all the time it is really a version. "I wonder," says Greswell, "what marks of a translation it should be expected to exhibit."[y]

Now, unless it be supposed that the imagined translator was under supernatural influence, and that by a miraculous agency his work had a special character attached to it,—a supposition which has never, so far as we know, been made,—we maintain, that the fact of its being *unlike* a translation, tends powerfully to support our argument, that it is *no* translation. For why should this immunity belong to *it?* Why should *it* be distinguished among all other works of the same kind, by wanting the marks

[w] Einl. § 46. [x] Introd. i. 75. [y] Harmony of the Gospels, i. 127.

of what, on the supposition, it really is,—a close and accurate version, and not, as we maintain, an original work? How has it happened, that, in this case, and in no other, the obvious marks of a translation have been escaped? and by what strange art (truly in this instance an *ars celare artem*) has this one translator succeeded in entirely concealing the real nature of his work, and in imparting to it the whole appearance and impress of an original?

Every one who has tried his hand at translation, knows how difficult it is to approach perfection in such a work. There are two things at which every good and faithful translator must aim. He must endeavour, in the first place, to come as near to literal exactness as possible; and he must take care, in the second place, not to sacrifice the idiom of the language into which his version is made. It must be his effort to give neither more nor less than the meaning of his author; to preserve the special characters of style and thought which appear in the original; and at the same time, to do no violence to the genius of the language into which he transfers it. And who has ever succeeded in perfectly accomplishing these two objects? What translator has not felt himself compelled, at times, to give a paraphrase rather than an exact version of his author, in order that he might avoid the intolerable awkwardness which a literal version would have caused? But nothing of this, as is confessed, appears in our existing Gospel of St. Matthew; and if, notwithstanding, it be in reality a translation, it can only be regarded as a sort of literary miracle, and one which is as unique as it is amazing; as solitary in kind, as it is exalted in degree.

"How can I read the Gospel of St. Matthew, as it now lies before me," asks Professor Stuart,[1] "and feel that I am reading a *translation* made in ancient times? Where is any *version* like it? The Septuagint? That is greatly diverse from it, in very many and important respects." In the truth of the statement here made we cordially concur; though, from its being unaccompanied with proofs, it is apt to produce little impression. It is not enough simply to declare, that "in very many and important respects," the Septuagint translation differs from our Greek Gospel of St.

[1] Notes to Fosdick's Hug, p. 710.

Matthew: in order to give any weight to the declaration, some specimens of such differences must be produced. We shall, therefore, notify a few particulars in which the difference may be observed, as these have occurred to us in reading over the Greek of Matthew, and comparing it with a book of the LXX, perused for this special purpose.

No portion of the Septuagint could more fairly be employed as a test in this inquiry, than the book of Genesis. Every scholar knows that the Pentateuch is by far the best executed part of the whole; and of the Pentateuch, no book approaches so nearly in simplicity of subject and style to Matthew, as does Genesis. Taking, then, the first book of the Old Testament in Greek, and comparing it with the first book of the New Testament in the same language, the one an acknowledged, the other an alleged translation from the Hebrew, such differences as the following are at once perceptible.

The paucity of the Hebrew language in conjunctions, and the very frequent use which is therefore made of the simple copulative, is well known. The "and" continually occurs in connecting clauses or sentences, where in Greek, which is so rich in particles, some other word would be employed. Now, we find this Hebrew usage copied very remarkably by the Greek translator, in Genesis, while in Matthew no such thing appears. On the contrary, our first Gospel is distinguished for the frequent occurrence in it of adverbs of time. While *καὶ* is continually made to do service in the Septuagint in the sense of "then," or "when," the proper adverb is as constantly employed in the Gospel. It has been observed, that *τότε* occurs no less than *ninety* times in Matthew,—a striking contrast, certainly, to the Greek translation of Genesis, in which that particle of time is scarcely ever used at all, but, as in the corresponding Hebrew, has its place usurped by the simple copulative.

Again, a well-known Hebrew idiom is that exemplified in Genesis xxv. 1, where the Hebrew literally translated, is, "And Abraham *adding*," etc. This is given by the Septuagint translator, "*προσθέμενος δὲ Ἀβραὰμ*," while no trace of such an awkwardness occurs in Matthew, but the equivalent Greek adverb, *πάλιν*, is employed.

Numerous other instances of a violation of the Greek idiom by the Septuagint translator, in order to approach the Hebrew mode of expression, might be mentioned. But let us only further notice such reduplications as *σφόδρα, σφόδρα* (Gen. vii. 19); such literal renderings as *ἤρεσαν οἱ λόγοι ἐναντιόν Ἐμμώρ* (Gen. xxxiv. 18),—evident marks of the translator, of which no examples are to be found in Matthew.

It is worthy of notice, moreover, that while peculiar *Greek* idioms scarcely appear at all in the Septuagint, there are some striking instances of such in our Gospel of St. Matthew. We shall refer only to chap. xxvii. 23, where we find a well-known idiomatic use of *γαρ* in the question of Pilate, *τί γὰρ κακὸν ἐποίησεν*; well rendered in our English version,—" *Why*, what evil hath he done?"

Nor can it be said, in answer to these remarks, that in the case of St. Matthew, there was a studied accommodation to the Greek idiom, while in the Septuagint, a simple effort was made to express the sense in a literal form, without any regard to the niceties of language. Neither assertion can be maintained. There is evidently no peculiar effort made in St. Matthew's Gospel, to approach to pure Greek expressions; on the contrary, it is written in exactly the same dialect as the other Gospels, and has, perhaps, a stronger Hebrew colouring than any of them. The writer manifestly did not aim at avoiding Hebraistic forms of expression, and yet he escaped those awkwardnesses which appear so frequently in the Septuagint, and even introduced occasionally, as we have seen, a peculiarly elegant and idiomatic Greek expression. All this is naturally and easily accounted for, on the supposition that he wrote originally in the Greek language, but Greek tinged, if we may so speak, by the Hebrew medium through which it passed.

And, on the other hand, it is plain that the translator of the Septuagint took the liberty, now and then, of avoiding the peculiar Hebrew mode of expression, when he felt that its literal counterpart would be ambiguous or absurd in Greek. Several examples of this have been noted by us in reading the book of Genesis: we shall only mention that which occurs in chap. xxxiv. 30. By turning to the English version, the peculiar Hebrew phrase here employed will be discovered, for it has most needlessly and offensively been retained by our translators.[a] But in the Septuagint, we find it rendered as follows:—μισητόν με πεποιήκατε, ὥστε πονηρόν με εἶναι πᾶσι τοῖς κατοικοῦσι τὴν γῆν. We see, then, that it was not from want of a desire to accommodate his work to the requirements of the Greek language, that the translator fell into those inelegancies which have been noticed. He manifestly felt the difficulty which every faithful translator must always feel—the difficulty of keeping close to the original, and yet not violating the idiom of the language in which he writes. Sometimes the one, and sometimes the other of these objects, is missed in the Septuagint, as in every other translation; and as neither the one error nor the other can be detected in our existing Greek Gospel of St. Matthew, we conclude that it is not a translated, but an original work.

(2.) We may next refer, in support of the proper originality of our existing Gospel, to *the manner in which citations from the Old Testament are made in it.*

St. Matthew is rich in quotations from the Old Testament. There are *thirteen* passages quoted from the Pentateuch, some of them oftener than once. There are *nine* citations from the Psalms. There are *sixteen* passages from the prophetical books,—eight of these from Isaiah, one from Jeremiah, and seven from the minor prophets. Now, if St. Matthew wrote in Hebrew, he would of course make his citations directly from the Hebrew text. And if his work was afterwards faithfully translated into Greek, the passages quoted would naturally be given in the form in which they stand in the Hebrew Bible. Such is the course which we would expect a scrupulously honest translator to have followed; and if we find that he tampered with his author in regard to citations, we have no security but he may have taken the same liberty in

[a] On the other hand, there are many instances in which the English version properly avoids the peculiar Hebrew phrase, while it is retained in the Septuagint. Thus, in Gen. xli. 1, we read in English, "and it came to pass at the end of two *full* years," where the Septuagint literally rendering the Hebrew has, δύο ἔτη ἡμερῶν. Thus difficult do translators feel it to avoid both the Scylla and Charybdis of this matter,—to preserve strict accuracy, and yet to write in accordance with the genius and laws of their own language.

many other respects; in short, unless it can be shown that the translator was himself inspired, we have, in such a case, no safeguard against his great and wilful dishonesty. There is one supposition, indeed, that will save his good faith, although we do find that the quotations, as he has given them, vary from the Hebrew Scriptures. He may have preferred adopting the Septuagint translation which was already current, to venturing on an independent translation of the Apostle's words. This course might, perhaps, be pardonable; but if he followed it, we would expect to find him consistent throughout, and that, by an application of this principle, we could explain all the variations which might appear in our present Gospel from the text of the Hebrew Scriptures.

How, then, stands the case? As every one may see on examining the Gospel, and comparing the quotations which it contains with the Hebrew original and the Septuagint translation, these are so made that if our Greek Gospel be a version from the Hebrew, it is impossible to explain them in consistency with the accuracy and fidelity of the translator. Some of the citations agree essentially with the Hebrew, but differ entirely from the Septuagint. Of this we have a remarkable example in chap. viii. 17, where the Evangelist completely departs from the Greek version, and develops, with a view to his special purpose, the Hebrew expressions. In other passages, again, there is an exact literal accordance with the Septuagint, as in xxi. 16, and that even in some cases, such as xix. 5, in which that translation differs to some extent from the Hebrew. There are also some passages, such as xii. 18–20, in which there is not an exact agreement observed either with the Greek or Hebrew; but an intensity is imparted by the Evangelist to the idea which he desires to bring out, and a somewhat different turn is given to the words by a departure from the *ipsissima verba* of the original text.

Now, how is it possible to explain these various phenomena on the supposition that our present Gospel is a translation? If it be regarded in that light, the utmost caprice appears in the conduct of the translator, and all confidence in his fidelity is destroyed. But if, on the other hand, we look at our present Greek Gospel of St. Matthew as the true, original work of an inspired Apostle, there is no difficulty in accounting for the differences observable in his mode of citation. We can easily conceive, in such a case, that the writer was led, as suited his purpose, to quote directly from the Hebrew, or exactly from the Septuagint, or even to depart to some extent from both, according as the Spirit who guided him might direct, and as the Apostolic authority which he possessed fully sanctioned.

There appears, then, a strong argument for the proper originality of the existing Greek Gospel in the manner in which quotations from the Old Testament are presented in it. As Hug has remarked (Introd. ii. § 12) "the Greek dress of the passages which are cited from the Old Testament is so managed, that their appearance must be ascribed to the author, and not to any translator." And some critics have been so impressed with this argument, that they have regarded it as in itself decisive of the question at issue. Thus Guerike declares, after acknowledging the force of the statements of antiquity, "Our existing Greek Gospel, however, truly bears in itself the sure sign and stamp also of originality. This appears especially from the fact that the citations which occur in it from the Old Testament do not harmonize throughout, all and wholly, either with the Hebrew text or with the Septuagint, but are given with so much freedom and peculiarity that they cannot be regarded as having flowed from a mere translator, nor can be explained on such a supposition."[b]

(3.) We may now class together several other corroborative proofs of the originality of our present Gospel, contenting ourselves with simply stating them, as to dwell upon them at any length appears altogether unnecessary.

There are the frequent explanations of Hebrew words and phrases which occur in our existing Greek Gospel (i. 23, xxvii. 46, etc.). These explanations could, of course, have had no place in the original; and when it is supposed, as Dr. Davidson and others find necessary,[c] that the translator added these clauses on his own authority, no security can be possessed that he did not make other

[b] Guerike, Isagog. § 14.

[c] It is a curious illustration of the difficulties of Dr. Tregelles' position, that he maintains (almost to absurdity) that such explanations formed part of the original *Hebrew* Gospel.

interpolations which seemed to him requisite or useful, and thus all confidence in his work is at an end.

Several Latinistic forms occur in our Greek Gospel which it seems in the highest degree improbable that a translator from Hebrew into Greek would have adopted. Thus, in v. 26, we find κοδράντης, *i. e.* the Latin *quadrans;* and in xxvii. 26, there occurs φραγελλόω, *i. e.* the Latin *flagello.* Now, as Townson well remarks on the first of these expressions, we may infer from its occurrence, that the Greek of this Gospel was the Apostle's own. Another, translating it from the Hebrew, would have taken the word that was best known to the Greeks, and have said λεπτὸν, as Luke does (xii. 59) when reporting the same statement. Dr. Davidson, indeed, appears to imagine that such forms were no translation, but had occurred in the original Aramaic of the Apostle. He says (Introd. i. 56), "The occurrence of Latin terms in the Gospel of Matthew will be reckoned no presumption that it was translated at Rome, when it is remembered that Matthew, as a tax-gatherer for the Roman government, must have come in contact, by the very nature of his office, with persons using the Latin language." But, as Townson again observes with respect to the use of the Latin term φραγελλόω (Matt. xxvii. 26), "If St. Matthew composed his Gospel first in Hebrew, he would not affect to Latinize his own tongue, but would declare the indignity suffered by Christ, as He had predicted it, which was certainly by a Hebrew word, when He said, 'They shall deliver Him to the Gentiles to mock and to scourge and to crucify Him.'" This seems to us decisive against those who believe, as Dr. Davidson does, that our Lord usually spoke in Hebrew. Certainly, in that case, St. Matthew, writing in the same language, would have used the Hebrew term which Christ himself employed, and would not have had recourse to a foreign tongue. "And who else," adds Townson, "would think of recurring to the Latin, when his business was to turn the Gospel into Greek, if it afforded him a proper term? But μαστιγοῦν is employed for scourging as a Roman punishment, both by secular authors and by the Evangelists, as St. John in the corresponding history, and by St. Mark, St. Luke, and even St. Matthew in reciting the prediction here mentioned. It seems, then, evident that φραγελλόω is not from the hand of a translator, but immediately of St. Matthew himself, whose intercourse with the Romans had made a word, which the Greeks did not acknowledge, familiar to him."[d]

It may also be noticed that the occurrence of the term ἰῶτα in the proverbial expression made use of by our Lord (chap. v. 18), does not suit well with the idea of a translation from the Hebrew, but seems to imply that the Greek is original. The use of such a proverb is also another proof, if such were needed, that our Lord was in the habit of *speaking* in Greek.

Moreover, on the supposition that our present Gospel is a translation from the Hebrew, made for the sake of Greek readers, it seems impossible to account for the retention of those Aramaic expressions which every now and then occur. Thus, to give only one example. We find the word κορβανᾶς, "the treasury," retained in the Greek, though that word must have been unintelligible to mere Greek readers. If St. Matthew himself was the writer of our Gospel, nothing could have been more natural than that he should employ this word, since, as Josephus tells us (Wars, ii. 9, 4), it was the common appellation in Palestine for the temple-treasury. But how one professing to translate this Gospel from Hebrew for the benefit of Greek readers should have retained this expression, seems impossible to conceive.

Again, every careful reader of the Greek text of St. Matthew must have noticed his very frequent use of the *imperfect* tense, and the peculiar delicacy of meaning which is thus oftentimes conveyed. For example: in chap. iii. 14, we read of John, with respect to Jesus, that he διεκώλυεν αὐτὸν, *i. e.* he not only "forbade" him, as it is in our English version, but rather, bringing out both the force of the preposition and the imperfect, "he continued earnestly to hinder him." At xviii. 30, also, we have a beautiful instance of the use of the imperfect, which is all the more marked in this case, as it is immediately followed by the aorist. The unmerciful servant "was not willing" (οὐκ ἤθελεν) to show compassion to his fellow-servant—such was his *continuing* state of mind—but he went out and cast (ἔβαλεν) him into prison, the tense here denoting an action at once definitely accomplished.

[d] Townson's Discourses on the Gospels, i. 172–3.

Now, such distinctions as these could scarcely be marked in the Hebrew or Aramæan, and would not, therefore, have been so carefully observed by one translating from that language.

Finally, it may, in our opinion, be urged as a strong proof of the proper originality of the Greek Gospel of St. Matthew, that expressions occur in it which could not have been given in Hebrew, or in the cognate dialects, *except by means of a circumlocution.* Thus we find the verb ἐπιορκέω employed in chap. v. 33, to denote the complex idea of "swearing falsely." There is no answering expression to this in the Hebrew or the Syriac. The Peschito renders the single Greek verb by two separate words, "thou shalt not be false in thine oaths;" and the Syriac of Cureton has "thou shalt not swear an oath of lying." The same thing may be said of the term παλιγγενεσία (chap. xix. 28). The amalgamated idea expressed in this single Greek word could be expressed only by two or more in Hebrew or Syriac. We find accordingly that the Peschito and Curetonian Syriac, while differing somewhat in their renderings, both agree in breaking up the one compound Greek term, and in seeking to convey its meaning by separate simple words. Now this appears plainly enough to indicate that our Greek Gospel is an original work. It is inconceivable that any translator should have condensed the more diffuse expressions of his original into the striking Greek terms which have been quoted. The tendency of every translator is much rather towards expansion than condensation. This is one of the necessities attending such a work, and will be found characteristic of every known translation. As, then, has been inferred respecting the Epistle to the Hebrews, that it must, in its present form, be an original work, from its containing Greek expressions which could only be expressed by a circumlocution in Hebrew,[e] so, for the same reason, we may conclude respecting our Greek Gospel of St. Matthew that it is an original and not a translated work.[f]

[e] Guerike says, regarding this Epistle, "Dem Briefe einzelne Worte für zusammengesetze eigen sind, die in Semitischen nur eine weitläufige Umschreibung ausdrücken vermag; z. B. πολυμερῶς und πολυτρόπως, μετριοπαθεῖν." Neut. Isag. § 25.

[f] We have taken no notice above of the *paronomasia* which is supposed to occur in chap. vi. 16. It requires too much search to find it to be of any

Altogether, it seems impossible to demonstrate *any* work to be original if that has not been done with respect to our present Gospel of St. Matthew. Every internal characteristic points, as we have seen, to that conclusion. The general character of the work—the manner in which citations occur in it—the several special features which may be marked in its structure and phraseology, all combine in leading us to the conclusion that it is an original and not a translated work. We have, moreover, found, on comparing it with the other synoptical Gospels, evidence of the same fact which it seems impossible to resist. It will be strange, indeed, if a work thus clearly shown on internal grounds to be original, should be destitute of external evidence to the same effect. We shall, in the following chapter, inquire whether or not that is the case. Meantime, we feel justified in saying, after the evidence which has already been adduced, that we should as soon be persuaded to believe that the Æneid of Virgil came not, in its present Latin dress, from the hands of its author, or that the Paradise Lost was really stolen by Milton from a poem in another language (as has been maintained, like many other false and erroneous *assertions*), as that our present Greek Gospel of St. Matthew issued not, in the form in which we now possess it, from the hands of the Apostle whose name it bears.

importance. Multitudes of better examples might be discovered in almost any translation; as, for instance, in our English Bible, at James i. 6. There might seem, to an English reader, a designed alliteration in "He that *wavereth* is like a *wave* of the sea;" but not the slightest trace of this is to be found in the original. Justly does Credner declare (§ 47), "That single wretched paronomasia (matte Wortspiel) is of no consequence whatever in shewing the Greek original of our present Gospel."

# CHAPTER IV.

## EXTERNAL EVIDENCE.

### SECTION I.—EXTERNAL EVIDENCE IN FAVOUR OF THE PROPER ORIGINALITY OF THE EXISTING GREEK GOSPEL OF ST. MATTHEW.

If we were to judge by the assertions which some of the defenders of the Hebrew original have made on this point, we should here feel ourselves utterly helpless. According to them, there is *no* external evidence that St. Matthew wrote a Gospel at all, unless it be admitted that he wrote in Hebrew. Thus says Dr. Tregelles, "On what ground do we believe that St. Matthew wrote a Gospel at all? Because we learn it from ancient and competent witnesses. But the same witnesses affirm that he wrote in Hebrew; and if endeavours be made to cast doubt on *this part* of their testimony, the whole (to say the least) is weakened."

Such statements occur very frequently in the writings of Dr. Tregelles, but we have no hesitation in saying that they are utterly without foundation. So far are they from giving a true account of the state of the case, that we propose in this section to prove all for which we need care in connexion with St. Matthew's Gospel, *without referring to any of the witnesses for the Hebrew original at all.* We do so, however, with a protest against the unfairness of the course, to which Dr. Tregelles endeavours to shut up the maintainers of the Greek original. It is plain from the language which he employs, that he too is not indisposed, when occasion serves, to adopt the *in terrorem* style of argument. As was remarked in the first chapter, there has been a too great looking at consequences by those who have argued for our present Gospel as a true original; and we there heartily joined with Dr. Tregelles in condemning the habit of being influenced by such considerations. But it is here evident that he exposes *himself*, though on other grounds, to the same condemnation. He attempts to frighten us from assigning their true historical value to the words of Papias and others, by declaring that, if we should in any measure discredit them, the consequences will be disastrous. We dare not, as he puts it, question the correctness of these writers on *one* point, lest we destroy their general trustworthiness, and thus invalidate the authority on which other important conclusions rest.

Now, we strongly protest against being fettered in this manner. We hold onrselves at perfect liberty to use the statements of the fathers, just as we do those of other ancient writers. We may, and *must*, discard all that we find in them which can be proved inconsistent with other known facts; and yet, at the same time, we may gratefully make use of them as positive witnesses to what there is otherwise no ground to question. No reason can be alleged why we should refuse to accept the statement of Papias, that St. Matthew was *the writer of a Gospel.* And we may surely receive his testimony to that fact, without being compelled also to believe on his authority, that the Gospel in question was written in Hebrew. It is utterly unphilosophical to demand, that if we refer to him at all, we must submit to his assertions or opinions on every point connected with the subject. *Totally accept, or totally reject*, cannot with any fairness be urged as the rule which is binding in such a matter. It is not the rule adopted with respect to the declarations of other ancient writers; and it is manifestly not the rule, by an application of which, any question that rests upon historic evidence can ever be settled.

Who shall demand, for instance, that we must either accept or reject *in toto* the statements contained in the first book of Livy's Roman history? Are we bound to deny that there ever was such a man as Romulus, if we refuse to believe the marvellous incidents which have been recorded of his birth and death? And may we not fully credit the general opinion that Numa Pompilius was a wise and sagacious prince, without believing that he acted under supernatural direction? May we not accept those statements of Livy which appear to be of a true historical character, without at the same time admitting all the legendary and mythical stories by which they are accompanied? The notion to the contrary is preposterous, and yet it is substantially this doctrine which Dr. Tregelles lays down with respect to Papias and other ancient ecclesiastical writers. We must receive *every thing* which they tell us, else we can avail ourselves of *nothing*. We must admit on their authority that St. Matthew wrote in Hebrew, or incur the penalty of not being able to learn from them that St. Matthew wrote at all! This is much the same as if we should be told, that, unless we acknowledge with Tacitus that Christianity is an "exitiabilis superstitio," we can make no use of that historian's statement, that our religion arose in Judæa in the reign of Tiberius, and that its Author bore the name of Christ! If this plan of dealing with ancient testimony were adopted, we might abandon as vain all attempts to distinguish between fact and fable, or to construct for ourselves from the records of the past a reliable account, either of human opinions or achievements.

We hold then that the maintainers of the Greek original are perfectly entitled, if they choose, to avail themselves of the testimony of Irenæus, Papias and others, to the effect that St. Matthew *did* write a Gospel, although they reject the statements of these writers as to the language in which that Gospel was composed. There may be no reason whatever for questioning the one statement, but every reason for receiving it. There may be, and as we have seen, there *is*, the plainest necessity for rejecting the other.

But to prove how groundless is Dr. Tregelles' allegation, we propose in this section to dispense entirely with the aid of the authors usually quoted in support of the Hebrew original, and independently of these, to show that we have external evidence that St. Matthew wrote our present Greek Gospel. We shall first bring forward evidence of the *authority*, and then of the *authorship;* shewing that it may both be proved that the Greek Gospel we now possess was always esteemed part of inspired Scripture, and that it was invariably attributed to the Apostle Matthew.

And here, we cannot do better than quote a passage from Dr. Tregelles himself. He says, "Even if we look at the Greek copy of Matthew *by itself*, we see that it must belong to *the Apostolic age*. The line of early writers who cite and use it, carry us back in the same way as they do with regard to Mark, Luke and John. The language too shows its origin as plainly as does that of the other three Gospels. . . . As to the canonical authority of the Greek Gospel which we possess, no further proof need (I believe) be given; we have the same evidence for this Greek translation which we possess for the original documents written by Mark, Luke and John. All four were used together by the church from the earliest days: all four have the same sanction."

We could not desire more than this with regard to the position of authority assigned to our present Greek Gospel. It has been transmitted to us as canonical Scripture from the earliest times. We can trace it to the Apostolic age. It occupies exactly the same footing with the other acknowledged books of the New Testament. All this Dr. Tregelles contends for in regard to our Greek Gospel viewed *by itself*, and yet he maintains the somewhat paradoxical position, that if we deny that St. Matthew wrote in Hebrew, we have no proof that he wrote at all!

We *have* proof at least that the Greek Gospel which goes under his name, is an apostolic and inspired document. That much it is granted may be proved independently of the statements made as to its Hebrew origin. Papias, the first writer who speaks of the Hebrew Gospel, does not carry us quite to the Apostolic age, and would not be enough to bear out the claims of our Greek Gospel, as these are stated above by Dr. Tregelles. But beyond him we can appeal to Polycarp and Ignatius, who both contain evident quotations from the Greek Gospel which we now possess.[g] Its authenticity then as canonical Scripture is clearly and confessedly established without the slightest aid being derived from those ancient writers that speak of its Hebrew original.

And next as to its authorship. Here too, we have the most satisfactory evidence without calling upon any of the assertors of the Hebrew original to bear their testimony. This Greek Gospel of ours, acknowledged to be in its present form Apostolic, has always, in that form, borne the name of St. Matthew. There is

[g] See the passages in Lardner, or in Jones on the Canon, or Guerike, Isagog. p. 124.

not a whisper in all antiquity of any rival claimant. In every existing MS., the most ancient as well as the most modern, the same name appears on its front. It is Matthew always, and Matthew only. The same thing holds with respect to every version of the New Testament, ancient and modern. One name is always prefixed, as that of the human author of this portion of Scripture. It is continually announced as the work of the Apostle Matthew. This is especially distinct in the most ancient version of all, the Peschito, which, as abundant evidence proves, must have been formed not later than the second century.[h] In this truly venerable and admirable translation, which thus approaches the Apostolic age, if indeed it does not completely reach it, the title of the first Gospel is, "*The Holy Gospel, the preaching of Matthew the Apostle.*" It will be observed that, in this inscription, there is no room left for those doubts which have sometimes been expressed with regard to the titles of this and the other Gospels, as they usually stand in the ancient MSS. It has, unreasonably we think, been doubted whether the common form *κατὰ Ματθαῖον*, can be held to denote true authorship. But in the title prefixed to this Gospel in the Peschito, all such ambiguity is precluded. It can only be interpreted as implying that the first Gospel proceeded from the pen of the Apostle, that it was *his* in the strict sense of being his proper authentic production. And thus, as it is almost universally admitted, and indeed cannot without contradicting the clearest evidence be denied, that the Peschito version was made directly from the Greek, we have the surest testimony both to the Apostolic antiquity of our existing Gospel of St. Matthew, and to the fact, that, from the very first, it was attributed to that Apostle.

Are we not then justified in styling the statements of Dr. Tregelles, on this point, without foundation? By a chain of the

[h] The extreme antiquity of the Syriac Peschito version is to our mind unquestionable. Attempts have indeed been made to render this point doubtful, but in vain. The single fact that this version did not originally contain those books of the New Testament which were for a time doubted of, is sufficient evidence of its high antiquity. Marsh assigns it to the middle of the second century, while Michaelis places it even in the first. See a very complete and satisfactory argument, in behalf of its almost Apostolic antiquity, in Jones on the Canon, i. 86-107.

clearest testimony we can demonstrate both the authority and the authorship of our first Gospel, without once referring to those fathers who assert its Hebrew original. How groundless then the allegation which Dr. Tregelles is so fond of making, "that if there is *any* evidence that St. Matthew wrote a Gospel at all, it is proved that he wrote it in what was then called Hebrew!" And may not even a somewhat stronger epithet be applied to such language as the following, which he is fond also of repeating? He says, "suppose it could be shown that we have no sufficient proof that St. Matthew wrote in Hebrew, would it follow that he must have written in Greek? This has been assumed by the advocates for a Greek original; but in fact if we get rid of early testimony, we are quite left in the dark as to the language. Why should not a claim be put in for other tongues besides Greek? Why not Latin or Coptic, etc.?"

This is utter recklessness, which carries in itself its own refutation. But it must be observed that it is a gross misrepresentation to insinuate respecting the defenders of the Greek original, that it is either their wish, or endeavour, to "get rid of early testimony." No such thing. They neither undervalue, nor do they in fact abandon it. They simply appeal from its mistakes to the evidence of unquestionable facts. And they gratefully accept of it and follow it, so far as it is not proved either self-contradictory, or opposed to what is otherwise indisputable. They gladly welcome all its statements, but they expect not to find these unmixed with error. They think themselves justified in sifting and trying all the declarations of the fathers by the principles of historical criticism, just as they do those of other ancient writers. To treat them otherwise, is not, in truth, to yield them a becoming respect, but to be guilty towards them of a childish superstition. There is nothing peculiarly sacred in their character as witness-bearers: they have no special claim to infallibility. And, as we scruple not to convict of error a Thucydides or Tacitus in particular statements which they make, while at the same time we do by no means slight or question their general testimony, so we are not to be accused of setting aside or seeking to disparage the testimony of the ancient fathers, simply because we refuse to pin our faith to every assertion which they make, and will not shut our eyes to the evidence of other undoubted facts in order that we may quietly rest in every one of their conclusions.

We accept then every declaration of antiquity which stubborn and resistless facts do not compel us to question. And by successive links of such testimony as there *is no cause* to question, we can trace up our existing Greek Gospel of St. Matthew to the very verge of the Apostolic age, find that it was always esteemed part of canonical Scripture, was quoted as the inspired and infallible word of God, and was with unanimous voice attributed to the author whose name it still bears.

Here we might stop; but at the risk of parting company with some who have accompanied us hitherto, we cannot help advancing a step farther. We are firmly convinced that the Greek Gospel of St. Matthew, as well as the other two synoptical Gospels, possesses direct *Apostolic* sanction. It appears to us certain from a careful examination of the evidence, both internal and external, that the Apostle John *saw* the other three Gospels before writing his own, and that by the nature of his own work, he has implicitly and intentionally *sanctioned* those of the three other Evangelists.

We are well aware that this is strongly controverted by some modern critics. But when we look into the Gospel of St. John, we think the evidence plain and irresistible. On no other supposition can we give any possible account of the special character which it possesses. The Apostle manifestly did not write for the purpose of furnishing us with a full history of the life of Christ, for many of the most important facts are altogether omitted, and in not a few instances, these are pre-supposed as already well known. He takes no notice of the birth, the baptism, the transfiguration, and many of the miracles of Christ recorded by the other Evangelists; while, at the same time, he assumes those things as quite familiar to his readers. Thus in chapter i. 32, there is a reference to the baptism of Christ, as reported by Matthew and Luke. In chap. ii. 1, the mother of Jesus is mentioned as a well-known person, although John himself has not previously noticed her. At chap. iii. 24, a parenthetical clause is inserted, apparently to guard against an error which might have arisen from the narrative of Matthew respecting the Baptist. And at chap. xx. 1, as Dr. Wordsworth has remarked in his work on Inspiration, the *stone* at the grave of Jesus is referred to, although John has not previously mentioned it: he says of the women, that they saw "the stone taken away," evidently supposing that his readers had learned, from the other Evangelists, regarding the tomb of Jesus, what he himself specially mentions of that of Lazarus, that "it was a cave, and a stone lay upon it."

The question then arises how St. John could have written in this manner,—on what ground he based the assumption which he manifestly makes, that both the facts which he has entirely omitted, and those to which he merely alludes, were quite familiar to his readers. Various opinions have been entertained on this subject. Eichhorn imagines, of course, that the Apostle wrote with an eye to the *Urevangelium*, and with the view of supplying its deficiencies. Lücke, Bleek, and Alford suppose that he took for granted the commonly received oral accounts. De Wette, again, says that St. John not only pre-supposed oral traditions, but also most probably the existence of, at least, *the Greek Gospel of St. Matthew.*

And with this latter view external testimony is coincident. We know of no reason why the statements of the ancient fathers on this point should be rejected. They are no doubt mixed up with errors, but after these have been set aside, (and *errors*, plainly demonstrated to be such, are all in ancient testimony that we would *ever* set aside), there seems to remain substantial and satisfactory evidence to the fact that St. John saw the first three Gospels before writing his own. There are, as Hug has remarked,[1] "internal evidences in the books of Matthew, Mark and Luke, that they were antecedent to the Gospel of John; and there are references in the latter which show that the writer was acquainted with the contents of the three other Gospels. Now, if the declarations of ancient writers coincide with this conclusion, they do not deserve to be so summarily rejected as they have been." And, as has been remarked, the external is, on this point, in perfect harmony with the internal evidence. Indubitable facts as to the

[1] Introd. ii. § 55.

lengthened period to which the Apostle John was spared upon the earth, and express testimonies of ancient writers as to the object which he had in view in writing his Gospel, tend to confirm the opinion which we derive from an inspection of the work itself. "The beloved disciple," says Dr. Wordsworth, "was providentially preserved to a great old age, not only to refute the heretics who denied the Lord that bought them, and to convince us of the Divinity of the *uncreated Word*, who was in the beginning with God, but also to *complete* the witness of the *written word*, and to vindicate its inspiration from the forgeries of false teachers, and to assure us of its fulness and divine character. In confirmation of this assertion, let us now refer to a fact attested by ancient and unexceptionable witnesses, (Clem. Al. apud Eus., vi. 14; Eus., iii. 24, etc.) Towards the close of his long life, copies of the three Gospels of St. Matthew, St. Mark and St. Luke, which, at that time, we are informed had been diffused throughout Christendom, were publicly brought to St. John in the city of Ephesus, of which he was the metropolitan, by some of the bishops of the Asiatic churches; and in their presence St. John openly acknowledged these three Gospels as inspired, and at their request composed his own Gospel, in order to *complete* the Evangelical record of the life and teaching of Jesus Christ."

John then saw and sanctioned the other Gospels.[k] Of that,

[k] We may here notice the objections of Alford to this opinion. His view is exactly opposite to that stated above. We have said that unless it be supposed that John knew of the other Gospels, no account can be given of the peculiar character attaching to his own; Alford, on the contrary, believes that "on such a supposition, the phenomena presented by his Gospel would be wholly inexplicable." He grounds this opinion on those parts, which this Gospel has in common with the other three. "And though," he says, "these are not so considerable in extent as in the case of the three Gospels, yet they are quite important enough to decide this question." But it should be noticed that in every part of the history in which John goes over the same ground with the other Evangelists, it is with quite a different purpose from theirs, and with the view of giving prominence to different incidents. Take *e.g.*, Chap. xiii., and compare it with the parallel passages in the other Gospels. Does it not manifestly take these for granted, inasmuch as it entirely omits all mention of the Eucharist, and leads us to contemplate the whole scene, as it were, from a different standpoint? And is not this quite in harmony with the opinion that St. John had seen the other Gospels, and had it in his view to supplement them?

both on internal and external grounds, there is every reason to be convinced. And thus, passing beyond Papias,—the most ancient authority to whom the advocates of the Hebrew original can appeal,—we carry our cause into the very presence of the beloved disciple. We ask the aged and venerable John, who has survived all his brethren in the Apostleship, what testimony *he* bears respecting those Gospels which had already been given to the church. And, in answer, he points to that inestimably precious work, which, as supplementary to these, he left as his great memorial to all coming generations. In his own Gospel he sets his seal upon those which had preceded it; he proceeds on the supposition that they are truthful and infallible records; and thus he affixes to all the three, the stamp of his Apostolic authority, and to the Greek of St. Matthew among the rest.

## SECTION II.—STATEMENTS OF ANCIENT WRITERS IN SUPPORT OF THE HEBREW ORIGINAL OF ST. MATTHEW'S GOSPEL.

We have seen that our present Greek Gospel of St. Matthew has been quoted as inspired Scripture from the Apostolic age, and that it has always been attributed to the person whose name it now bears. We have also seen, that there is demonstrative evidence in the Gospel itself, especially when viewed in connexion with the others, that it is an original and not a translated work; coming as certainly in its present form from the hands of St. Matthew, as the other two issued in their present form from the hands of St. Mark and St. Luke.

If these points have not been established to the satisfaction of the reader, our argument has failed, and we cannot now retrieve our position. And, unless we have succeeded in making good our own hypothesis with respect to the question at issue, it would truly be thankless toil to seek to damage that of our opponents. We might much rather, in such a case, leave the defenders of the Hebrew original quietly to repose in the fancied security of their position, and need not take upon ourselves, the ungracious task of exposing its weakness and insufficiency.

And, on the other hand, if the points mentioned have been

settled, as is believed, on grounds which cannot be set aside, the hostile assertions of either ancient or modern writers need cause us very little trouble. Facts, once ascertained, remain facts, however much they may be mistaken or controverted; and it matters little how weighty may be the authorities that question them, or how numerous the writers who contradict them. No one, for example, thinks it worth while, at the present day, elaborately to refute the assertions of early heathen writers, respecting the manner in which the worship of the primitive Christians was conducted. Though Tacitus evidently believed the stories in circulation on this point, and lent them the sanction of his great name,[1] the facts of the case are too well known to us from other sources, to allow these assertions, numerous as they are, and weighty as is the authority of some that make them, to produce any impression upon our minds. The most that we seek to do, is to give some probable explanation of the manner in which they may have arisen. And whether we succeed in effecting this or not, the conclusion already formed as to their erroneousness cannot be shaken. That rests on independent and irrefragable evidence. It is implied in all that proves Christianity to be from God; and as long as that fact is admitted, it is rather a curious question about the vagaries to which the

[1] In the well-known chapter (Annal. xv. 44) in which he says of the Christians that they were "per flagitia invisi," and while acquitting them of the particular crime of setting fire to the city, with which Nero, for purposes of his own, had charged them, nevertheless brands them as being distinguished for their "general hatred of mankind" (odio humani generis). On these expressions of the Roman historian, Brotier remarks, "Crimini datum, quod seditiosi, jamque repressi, rursus *erumperent*, eâ superstitione imbuti, quæ deos, terrarum dominos, imperii secundarumque rerum auctores, non modo non veneraretur, sed impiis etiam dicteriis lacesseret: quæ deorum cultores, morte dignos, æternisque ignibus devovendos, furioso *generis humani odio* pronuntiaret: dum ipsi *per flagitia invisi*, publicos optimosque mores aversati, soli mortalium, nec templa, nec aras, nec sacrificia haberent; secretos tantum et legibus prohibitos, conventus nocturnos frequentarent, in quibus fœdarentur horrendis impudicitiarum spurcitiis, Thyestæisque pascerentur dapibus." These horrible accusations had arisen from some confused and erroneous ideas of Baptism and the Lord's Supper which had found their way in among the heathen, and which being once set in circulation, it was found no easy matter to counteract and check. Thus readily are false statements propagated, and even rise at times to the dignity of history, when they are made with respect to matters which of necessity were at first ill understood.

human mind is liable, than any inquiry of moment to us as Christians, while we seek to trace to their origin these mistakes of heathen writers.

And so with regard to the passages usually quoted from the fathers, in opposition to the proper originality of our Greek Gospel of St. Matthew. If that point has already been made out by evidence of its own, which is completely sufficient, we have simply to offer some possible explanation of the counter-statements that have been made upon the subject. And whether we succeed in showing these statements to be palpable errors, or to be the fruit and consequence of other errors; or whether we fail in revealing such as their true character, in either case, the fact already proved will remain as certain and immoveable as ever.[m]

We proceed, then, to a brief examination of the well-known passages in the ancient fathers, which bear upon the question at issue. These have often been held as in themselves decisive of the controversy; and yet, we believe, there is not one of them but may be shown to be either absurd, ambiguous, doubtful in point of authority, or contradictory to other declarations of the writer in which it is found.

We begin with the famous saying of Papias, preserved by Eusebius (Eccl. Hist. iii. 39), to the effect, that "Matthew wrote the oracles in the Hebrew dialect, and each one interpreted them as he was able."[n] This is the very corner-stone in the argument of those who plead for a Hebrew original. Papias was Bishop of Hierapolis, in Phrygia, in the beginning of the second century, and is thus a witness of undoubted antiquity. But we must

[m] Dr. Tregelles lays down the following somewhat singular logical canon as necessary to be observed by all those who adopt the view which we have taken of the question under discussion. "To maintain," he says, "the Greek original, there ought to be, 1st, a refutation of the evidence advanced in favour of the Hebrew; 2nd, at least equal evidence in favour of the Greek; and 3rd, a proof that such evidenee is equally congruent with the facts of the case." We have willingly assumed the *onus probandi* in the controversy, but we could scarcely be expected to do that and at the same time begin with a refutation of the arguments opposed to our proposition. It is sufficient to notice these now, after the proofs on which we rest have been brought forward, and the conclusion to which they lead established.

[n] Ματθαῖος μὲν οὖν Ἑβραΐδι διαλέκτῳ τὰ λόγια συνετάξατο· ἡρμήνευσε δ' αὐτὰ ὡς ἦν δυνατὸς ἕκαστος.

receive all that he says with caution; for the very writer who has conveyed to us an acquaintance with some of his sentiments, does so with the accompanying statement,—that he was "a man of very little understanding" (*σφόδρα σμικρὸς τὸν νοῦν*). And there is enough in the specimens which the historian has preserved of his sentiments, to show us that this judgment was just. Some very foolish stories are reported by Eusebius, as having been credited by Papias, and some very silly opinions are attributed to him: but we may restrict ourselves to the statement more immediately before us, and we shall find, even in it, evidence sufficiently plain of the weakness of his understanding. For, let us endeavour to attach any common-sense meaning to the words which have been quoted, and we shall find that impossible. We may admit that *λόγια* certainly means the whole Gospel narrative, and that *ἡρμήνευσε* denotes "translated" (both of which points have, without reason, as appears to us, been doubted); but what shall we make of *ἕκαστος*? "*Every one*," says Papias, translated the Hebrew Gospel to the best of his ability; and of whom is this statement made? does it refer to Jews or Gentiles? If to Jews, then why did they translate this Gospel, when, *ex hypothesi*, it was written for them in their own language, just that they might need no translation? And if, on the other hand, *ἕκαστος* be regarded as referring to Gentiles, how did it come to pass that they were *able* to translate the Hebrew at all? Is it not a well-understood fact, that so rare was an acquaintance with that language in ancient times, that very few even of the teachers of the church understood it? Papias himself, in all probability, did not know a word of Hebrew; and in that respect, at least, he was not inferior to the great majority of his fellow-Christians. But where, then, the "every one" who translated this supposed Hebrew Gospel? In what country, or among what class, shall we seek for those who were both qualified, and found it necessary, to translate the Hebrew Gospel of St. Matthew? The only answer we receive to these questions, is the following from Dr. Davidson (Introd. i. 69):—"Those who had the Aramæan document in their hands, endeavoured as well as they could to ascertain its meaning; which, they being Greeks (for *ἕκαστος* must be restricted to persons, to whom, like Papias himself, the Hebrew was not vernacular), best did by translating it to themselves." The "every one" of Papias, then, is to be sought only among the Greeks. That being the case, we have several questions to ask, and to which we shall be glad to obtain answers. *First*, What reason is there to think that a knowledge of Hebrew was so common among those Christians, in the early age, to whom, like Papias himself, that language "was not vernacular," that "every one" of them could be said to translate for himself from a Hebrew document? Is there the slightest evidence that the language of Palestine ever became generally, or even, except most rarely, known to Greek-speaking nations? Is not the very opposite universally admitted? and where, then, the "every one" who translated the supposed Hebrew Gospel? *Secondly*, Why should the *Greeks* have laboured so hard to translate this narrative of St. Matthew, when their wants were specially provided for in the Gospels of St. Mark and St. Luke, and when the Gospel of St. Matthew was, on the supposition of our opponents, not intended or fitted for them at all? It was *par excellence* the Hebrew Gospel; and why, then, should the Gentiles have struggled so industriously to extract some meaning from a document, which, by the mere fact of its being written in Hebrew, it was supposed that they did not require? Will it be said, that it was only till the Gospels of St. Mark and St. Luke were published, that the Greeks thus laboured to translate into their own language the Hebrew Gospel, and that after these were given to the world their efforts ceased? Then we ask, *Thirdly*, How comes it to pass, that, if the whole Christian world were dependent for a time on a Gospel in the Hebrew language, and if, as was natural in such circumstances, they strove to the utmost to understand it,—if, in short, the Hebrew Gospel of St. Matthew was, during many years, in every body's hands as the sole authoritative account of the Christian faith, how comes it to pass, in such a case, that no trace of it whatever has been preserved in the writings of antiquity, at least out of Palestine? Is it conceivable, that a Gospel which, for a time, was *every one's* Gospel, should have perished so utterly, that no relic of it has survived? If the Gentile Christians generally did, as Dr. Davidson supposes, for a series of years, derive their information respecting their religion from an inspired book written in Hebrew by the Apostle Matthew, can we believe that it would so easily and entirely have been suffered to fall into oblivion? When it is conceived that the Hebrew Gospel of St. Matthew was confined to Palestine, some plausibility may be given to the notion, that, although an inspired book, it was suffered to sink into obscurity, because never known, nor intended to be known, by the Christian world at large. But when it is maintained, that "every one" among the Gentiles was for a considerable period in the habit of translating it, the speedy and complete oblivion into which it was permitted to fall, becomes utterly inexplicable. The very difficulty which Greek readers felt in making out its meaning, must have impressed its statements all the more upon their minds; and it is, in such a case, totally incredible, that the wave of forgetfulness should so soon and effectually have passed over their memories, and obliterated every impression which had been produced by their hard and constant study of that Hebrew document.

Thus, it appears to us, that the statement of Papias, looked at in whatever light, is replete with folly; and comes to us most naturally, as the saying of one who, while doubtless possessed of many valuable qualities, is certified as having been a man of easy credulity, and scanty judgment.

The next testimony is that of Irenæus (Hær. iii. 1), in the following terms:—"Matthew also issued a Gospel among the Hebrews in their own dialect, while Peter and Paul were preaching at Rome, and laying the foundations of the church there."[o] This statement can scarcely be regarded as possessed of any independent value. So far as the language in which St. Matthew's Gospel was written is concerned, it is little more than the echo of Papias. We know, from Eusebius, that Irenæus was a great follower of

[o] The Greek of Irenæus, as preserved by Eusebius (Eccl. Hist. v. 8), is as follows: Ὁ μὲν δὴ Ματθαῖος ἐν τοῖς Ἑβραίοις τῇ ἰδίᾳ διαλέκτῳ αὐτῶν καὶ γραφὴν ἐξήνεγκεν εὐαγγελίου. The attempt which has been made by Hales, Robinson (Theol. Dictionary), Wordsworth, etc., to interpret the καὶ in this passage as implying the publication of *two* Gospels, appears to me vain. The meaning simply is, that St. Matthew, after *preaching* to the Hebrews, *also* published a Gospel in their dialect. The date assigned for this alleged fact (A.D. 61–63) seems as erroneous as the fact itself is mis-stated. The early publication of St. Matthew's Gospel (A.D. 37–41) appears to admit of no question.

that father, on account of his antiquity; and as he adopted Millenarian notions simply because these had been espoused by a man that had known Polycarp, whom he so much venerated, there is reason to believe that, in like manner, he embraced this opinion respecting the original language of St. Matthew, simply because he found it in the writings of Papias.

And thus the erroneous report which had originated with that ancient, but far from reliable witness, spread and was propagated in the church. "Writers," says Bolingbroke, "copy one another; and the mistake that was committed, or the falsehood that was invented, by one, is adopted by hundreds."[p] We find, accordingly, that Papias had many followers. Origen, Eusebius, Epiphanius, Jerome, etc., all repeated the statement, which rests, as its ultimate foundation, on the testimony already considered; and by giving heed to it, they were, as we shall see, betrayed into various difficulties and inconsistencies.

But, before proceeding to notice the statements of these writers, we must glance at the account given us of another, who is deemed an independent witness. Eusebius (Hist. Eccl. v. 10) contains the following passage respecting Pantænus:—"Pantænus is said to have visited the Indians, where, according to report, he found the Gospel of Matthew in use, before his arrival, among the Christians there, to whom Bartholomew, one of the Apostles, had preached, and who left them the Gospel of Matthew written in Hebrew letters," etc. Now, not to speak of the intrinsic improbability of this statement, it is sufficient to observe the hesitating way in which the historian reports it. The account is very far from having the weight of direct testimony. Pantænus is *said* to have gone where it is *said* he found the Hebrew Gospel.[q] And thus it is with the supposed Aramaic original of St. Matthew's Gospel as with the many stories of apparitions which have been palmed upon the world. Multitudes are ready to avouch the fact, but it is almost always on the authority of some one else. There is no such thing as direct personal testimony. One believes because another believed, and that other because he had it from a

[p] Letters on the Study of History, v. § 4, quoted by Professor Norton, i. 2.

[q] The Greek here is, λέγεται, ἔνθα λόγος εὑρεῖν.

third whose veracity could not be questioned. But still the person who actually *saw* with his own eyes the marvellous appearance remains undiscovered, and seems to conceal himself all the more obstinately the more his testimony is demanded or desired. And so is it with respect to the Hebrew original of St. Matthew's Gospel. That is the spectre which haunts ecclesiastical antiquity. Many speak of it and assure us of its reality, but *no one ever saw it.* The most that we hear of it is, that some one else had met with it, until at last we are introduced to the credulous Papias himself, who is exactly the man to become the father of a *ghost story*, and to whose weak judgment, we believe, the whole delusion is to be ascribed. Be explained as it may, the testimony of Pantænus, as reported by Eusebius, dwindles down almost to nothing, and is presented to us in such a cautious way by the historian that it almost appears as if he did not wish us to believe it.

The next witness is the accomplished Origen. And here, at length, we meet with one who is thoroughly competent to give plain and decided evidence in favour of the Hebrew original, supposing it had ever existed. Well skilled in Hebrew learning, enthusiastic in sacred studies, earnest and careful in searching out everything that could illustrate the sacred Scriptures, Origen was the very person to find this Hebrew Gospel if it was to be found, or to preserve to us some traces of its peculiar character if it had ever been in existence. And he was well acquainted with the leading Christians in Palestine; so that, as he was sure to desire a sight of the Hebrew Gospel among them, if he really believed it to be that of the Apostle, he was equally sure of having his desire most readily gratified. His friends in Palestine would have been delighted to furnish him with any books of Scripture which they might possess in a peculiar form, and we know too much of his habits of mind not to be sure that he would ask them. Origen was as likely as any modern critic to be interested and excited by the idea of St. Matthew's original Gospel being in existence in Hebrew, and would undoubtedly have sought after it had he believed that it was to be found. But, unfortunately for the defenders of the Hebrew original, so little dependence did this learned father place upon the tradition upon which they build so much, that he seems at times to have utterly forgotten its existence. Thus, in his treatise "on Prayer," he observes, in his exposition of the fourth petition of the Lord's prayer, that "the Greek word ἐπιούσιος is not used by any of the learned, nor by the common people, but seems to have been framed by the Evangelists, for *both Matthew and Luke* agree in using it without any difference." Here he seems completely oblivious of the fact that St. Matthew's Greek Gospel was said to be a translation; and it is only when his mind is specially turned to the subject, that he remembers to state his "having learned by tradition that the Apostle wrote in Hebrew."

The same remarks will apply to Eusebius. Sometimes he seems quite to forget that there was any report current as to the Greek Gospel of St. Matthew being a translation from the Hebrew. At other times he recalls the tradition which prevailed to that effect, and writes accordingly. Referring to the peculiar manner in which a quotation from the Hebrew is made by the Evangelist (Matt. xiii. 35), he tells us that "Matthew, being a Hebrew, made use of his own *interpretation*[r] of the original (ἐρεύξομαι, etc.), instead of adopting that of the Septuagint (φθέγξομαι, etc.)." Here it is clearly implied that, in the estimation of Eusebius, St. Matthew himself was the author of our present Greek Gospel; while, in another place, we find him attributing a particular Greek expression which occurs in it (ὀψὲ σαββάτων), not to the Apostle, but to the person who translated his work from the Hebrew.

Now, such confusion of thought and statement on this subject is quite compatible with the idea that there was a tradition widely diffused in the church that St. Matthew wrote in Hebrew, but seems inexplicable if that tradition were accepted as embodying an indubitable truth. Impressed at times, as would appear, by the striking evidence of originality which the Gospel itself contains, the fathers

[r] We are perfectly aware of the different views which have been taken of the word ἔκδοσις employed by Eusebius in this passage. Davidson assigns it the meaning "recension;" but that this is incorrect, and that "translation" is its true rendering appears from the words of Eusebius himself in the very same passage. He immediately uses ἐκδέδωκεν in the sense of "translated," and this is quite sufficient to fix the meaning of ἔκδοσις as given above.

write as if they had never heard it was a translation; and then again, falling under the influence of the prevailing tradition, they write as if they did not regard our present Greek Gospel as an original, while, at the same time, they continue to quote it as inspired Scripture.

We must now glance at the position occupied by Jerome in this controversy. And here we find "confusion worse confounded." At one time Jerome writes as if he had actually seen the long-hidden Hebrew Gospel of St. Matthew. He says (de Viris illus., 3), "Ipsum Hebraicum habetur usque hodie in Cæsariensi bibliotheca, quam Pamphilus martyr studiosissime confecit. Mihi quoque a Nazaræis qui in Beræa urbe Syriæ hoc volumine utuntur, describendi facultas fuit." But again he says (Comm. in Matt. ii.), "In Evangelio quo utuntur Nazaræi et Ebionitæ, quod nuper in Græcum de Hebræo sermone transtulimus, et *quod vocatur a plerisque* Matthæi authenticum." And as the latest testimony which he bears on this subject, he says (adv. Pel. iii.), respecting this same Gospel that was in use among the Nazarenes, that it was entitled, "secundum Apostolos, *sive ut plerique autumant*, juxta Matthæum."

Now, without entering at any length into the consideration of these and other passages in Jerome, it is plain that the longer that father investigated the subject, the more doubtful he became as to the claims of the Gospel of the Hebrews to be regarded as the original work of the Apostle Matthew. He found that the canonical Greek Gospel and the existing Hebrew one varied very materially in a multitude of passages. So great indeed was the diversity between them, that Jerome thought it worth his trouble to translate the Ebionite Gospel into Greek. This one fact demonstrates the essential difference which must have existed between the pretended Hebrew original of Matthew and the Greek Gospel which has always gone under his name. And the accounts which have been transmitted to us of that Hebrew Gospel, as well as the specimens which have been preserved of its contents, prove that it would be an abuse of language in any sense to identify it with our existing Gospel of St. Matthew. It both wanted much which is found in the Greek, and contained much which that does not possess. As an example of its omissions, it is sufficient to state, on the authority of Epiphanius, that (in some copies at least) the first two chapters were entirely wanting; as an example of the additions which it contained, we may give the following, which Jerome quotes from it, respecting our Lord's baptism: "Factum est autem, quum ascendisset Dominus de aquâ, descendit fons omnis Spiritus Sancti et requievit super eum ac dixit ei; Fili mi, in omnibus prophetis expectabam te, ut venires et requiescerem in te, tu es enim requies mea, tu es filius meus primogenitus, qui regnas in sempiternum." With all these differences there were, no doubt, many passages common to both the Greek and Hebrew Gospels; but whether we judge from the quotations out of the Hebrew document which have been preserved by ancient writers, or by the fact of Jerome having taken the trouble to translate it, we must hold that it was an essentially different work from our existing Greek Gospel of St. Matthew.[s] The mere existence, however, of this corrupt Hebrew Gospel served to fortify the tradition already prevalent in the church that St. Matthew wrote originally in that language. The Jewish sectaries in Palestine eagerly took advantage of the existing tradition to claim for their heretical Gospel the distinction of being the original work of the Apostle; and they succeeded in persuading some of the fathers that such was its real character. Epiphanius was completely deceived; and Jerome also was so for a time. But this latter father, as we have seen, became more and more uncertain as to the claims of the Ebionite Gospel, the longer his attention was directed to the subject; and in his latest written works virtually retracts the testimony he had borne as to its identity with the original of St. Matthew, and leaves that opinion to rest on the authority of others.[t]

[s] See the passages of the Hebrew Gospel which have been preserved in ancient writers collected by Dr. Davidson, Introd. i. 17–29.

[t] Credner (Einl. § 45) thus writes respecting the view which Jerome at last adopted respecting the Gospel of the Hebrews: "Hieronymus, welcher, wie andere Gelehrte damaliger Zeit, in demselben den Grundtext zu unserem Matthäus suchte, erklärte nach jahrelanger Bekanntschaft, Prüfung und Uebersetzung desselben *zuletzt* (im Jahre 415): 'In evangelio juxta Hebræos, quod Judaico quidem sermone, sed Hebraicis literis scriptum est, quo utuntur usque hodie Nazareni, secundum apostolos, sive, *ut plerique autumant*, juxta Matthæum, quod et, etc.' Diese letze Erklärung des Hieronymus steht als entscheidend über allen frühern. Hieronymus fand den Urtext zu unserem Matthäus in diesem Ev. nicht."

We have shown, then, that the source of the whole confusion which pervades antiquity with respect to the original language of St. Matthew's Gospel is to be found in a statement of the weak and gossiping Papias. And when we remember that that father was unacquainted with Hebrew, as well as deficient in judgment, we can easily conceive how his mistake may have occurred. He, no doubt, heard it stated that St. Matthew wrote in Palestine with a special reference to the Hebrew Christians, and how naturally, then, would such a man conclude that the Apostle must have written in the Hebrew tongue! He tells us, accordingly, "Matthew wrote the oracles in the Hebrew dialect;" and then, perceiving the difficulty which this statement involved with respect to Gentile readers, he adds, (as we think his words may be supplemented in full accordance with what we know of the *very* simple character of the man,) "If you ask me how those who were not natives of Palestine dealt with this Gospel in Hebrew, and how *they* contrived to extract any instruction from it—why, 'each man translated it as well as he could!'"[u]

[u] It seems not improbable from the aorist here employed (ἡρμήνευσεν) that Papias himself possessed the Gospel of St. Matthew in Greek. He speaks of the time for "every one" translating as past; and this seems to imply that, in his day, no need was felt for such translations. But although his words may warrant the inference that he himself possessed the Gospel of St. Matthew in Greek, they furnish no hint (as Thiersch and others have argued) that the *Apostle himself* published a Greek translation of his work, or even that the Greek *is* a translation.

It may here be noticed, in illustration and confirmation of the hypothesis above stated as to the manner in which the error of Papias may have originated, that the same cause has been at work, and the same effect has to some extent followed, with respect to the Gospel of St. Mark. An idea, right or wrong, prevailed in the church that Mark wrote at Rome, and specially for the Romans; and from this the inference was drawn that he must have written in their own language, *i. e.* in Latin. We find this stated at the end of the Peschito version of St. Mark's Gospel; and what was a natural inference for a writer in Syria to draw with respect to St. Mark was equally natural for a writer in Phrygia with respect to St. Matthew. Both writers were probably ignorant of the fact that *Greek* was the reigning language in Rome as well as Palestine, and were thus betrayed into error. And had this opinion respecting St. Mark been generally disseminated in the church at a sufficiently early period, it seems not unlikely that it might have prevailed as extensively as did the tradition regarding St. Matthew. Papias being one of the first who collected historical notices on those points which were so interesting to

With regard to the Gospel according to the Hebrews—otherwise called the Hebrew Gospel of St. Matthew—otherwise the Gospel of Peter—otherwise still, and more pompously, the Gospel of the twelve Apostles,—it is not difficult to account for its origin. The Jewish Christians who remained in Palestine after the destruction of Jerusalem by the Romans, were soon divided into two sects, both zealous for the law, though in different degrees. These were the Ebionites and Nazarenes; of whom the former held, among other very erroneous tenets, that the law of Moses was *universally* binding, while the latter, with a nearer approach to orthodoxy in general, maintained that it was obligatory only on *Jewish* Christians. The Jewish prejudices of these sects led them to prefer that their sacred books should be read in the Hebrew language. Some of the New Testament Scriptures were therefore early translated from the Greek, and used, not from necessity, as Dr. Tregelles supposes, but from bigotry, in the peculiarly Jewish dialect. And the Gospel of St. Matthew having been written in Palestine, and primarily intended for the Christians of that country, naturally obtained the first place in their estimation. A version of it had been made from the original Greek into Hebrew at a very early period; and, with many omissions and interpolations, it continued in the time of Jerome to be used by those Judaic Christians, and was by them often boasted of and referred to as the supposed original of St. Matthew's Gospel.[x]

Such, then, is the simple explanation which we propose of the perplexities and contradictions which appear on this subject among the ancient fathers of the church. And for any one, on the ground of such statements as those which have been considered, to set up the claims of a Gospel which cannot be said with certainty ever to have been seen by any one, and which has left no

all Christians, was necessarily much deferred to and followed. Eusebius, in referring to his millenarian views, tells us that there were many who espoused his sentiments simply *from a regard to his antiquity*; and the same cause, doubtless, operated in procuring such a wide and general acceptance for his statement respecting the original language of St. Matthew.

[x] See a valuable note on the Gospel according to the Hebrews, by Professor Stuart, in Fosdick's translation of Hug's Introduction, p. 700.

trace of its existence in the church, against the claims of another Gospel which has been acknowledged as inspired from the earliest age, which has been constantly appealed to as the genuine production of the Apostle Matthew, from which all known versions—even the earliest—have been made, and which bears in itself the proof of its own originality,—appears to us to be the perverting of all evidence, and the turning of criticism into foolishness.

## SECTION III.—REMARKS ON CURETON'S SYRIAC GOSPELS.

It has been observed in the preceding section, that notwithstanding all that is said by the ancient fathers, of the Hebrew Gospel of St. Matthew, it is extremely doubtful (to say the least) whether any one of them believed that he had ever seen it. But in this publication of Dr. Cureton, we are ourselves promised an approach towards that gratification. The learned editor of these Remains does not, indeed, quite claim that they contain part of the veritable original of St. Matthew, but he uses the following sufficiently exciting language: that this Syriac copy has "pretensions to be considered as more nearly representing the exact words of St. Matthew himself, than any other yet discovered."

This statement, if substantiated, would of necessity make an important change in the question which has engaged our attention. We should be furnished with a real, existing rival to our present Greek Gospel, and no longer tantalized by hearing continually of a Hebrew original, which eludes all attempts at identification or discovery. There must, however, be the clearest evidence to establish the claim which Dr. Cureton puts forth in behalf of his recent publication. We must have the plainest proof, that the true original of St. Matthew, so long missing, has at last approximately been found; and such proof, as we shall now endeavour to show, the present work of Dr. Cureton utterly fails to produce.

Dr. Cureton's argument proceeds on the assumption that St. Matthew's Gospel was originally written in Hebrew:—"In the preceding observations upon the text of St. Matthew," he says

(p. lxxiii), "it will be seen that I have assumed that his Gospel was originally written in the Hebrew dialect, generally spoken by the Jews in Palestine, at the time when the events took place of which it furnishes the narrative. I have done this, upon the conviction that no fact relating to the history of the Gospels is more fully and satisfactorily established." If, then, we have succeeded in the previous chapters, in showing that St. Matthew did *not* write in Hebrew, but in Greek, the argument of Dr. Cureton is, in this point of view, entirely set aside. Instead of rejoicing with him, that now, after being buried in oblivion for almost the whole period of our era, something like the original Gospel of St. Matthew has at last been discovered, we can hold to the conviction, that the genuine work of the Apostle has been in the hands of the church from the beginning, and is still possessed by us, in that simple Greek text with which we are all familiar.

But there is something more than assumption in Dr. Cureton's work, and in this is found the reason which induces us to notice it at all. If he simply took for granted that St. Matthew wrote in Hebrew, and built up his theory on that supposition, we might, without another word, leave his argument to be judged of by the considerations which have been adduced in the preceding chapters. But, while proceeding on the assumption mentioned, he professes also to find confirmatory evidence for it, in the comparison which he institutes between the Greek and Syriac texts, and in various considerations which, he thinks, result from such a comparison. Thus, after referring to those passages in the fathers, which are usually quoted in support of the Hebrew original, and stating, that "such a chain of historical evidence appears amply sufficient to establish the fact, that St. Matthew wrote his Gospel originally in the Hebrew dialect of the time," he adds (p. lxxiv), "a careful and critical examination of the Greek text of this Gospel will afford very strong confirmation of this." The same result, he believes, follows from the comparison which he makes between this Syriac fragment, and the passages which have been preserved to us of the Gospel according to the Hebrews. "This comparison," he writes (p. lxxxviii), "by proving the agreement between the two, tends also to confirm the historical testimony, as to the fact that St. Matthew originally wrote his Gospel in Hebrew or Syro-Chaldaic, and that the Gospel according to the Hebrews was often taken for the authentic work of the Apostle."

Since, then, Dr. Cureton conceives, that on various grounds he can derive support from the Syriac recension of St. Matthew, for the opinion that the Apostle wrote originally in the cognate language, it is necessary to the completeness of our argument, that we enquire into the validity of those grounds on which he rests. This cannot here be done at any great length, nor will that appear needful. The first firm grasp which is taken of Dr. Cureton's arguments is sufficient utterly to crush them. The whole fabric which he attempts to build, out of mingled assumptions and proofs, in support of the claims of this Syriac copy of St. Matthew, becomes a heap of ruins the moment that we touch it; and the Greek text is left still without a rival, and is more clearly proved to be the authentic work of the Apostle than ever.

The question, then, is just this: Whether it is our common Greek Gospel, or this Syriac text, which appears to be the translated work; for, of course, if one be held an original, the other must immediately take rank as a translation. Dr. Cureton very confidently maintains, that the Greek exhibits unmistakeable proofs of being a translation from the Hebrew; we as confidently maintain that the Syriac is plainly a translation from the Greek.

The manner in which Dr. Cureton endeavours to make good his position, is by pointing out in the differences which exist between the Syriac copy and the Greek, evident traces of error, as he thinks, on the part of the Greek translator, from his having mistaken one Hebrew word for another. He takes it for granted (p. lxxx), "that the original Gospel of St. Matthew, although composed in Syro-Chaldaic, the vernacular tongue of the Hebrew people in Palestine at that time, was, nevertheless, written in Hebrew characters, similar to those still used by the Jews." He supposes, then, that the Apostle employed the square form of the Hebrew letters still in common use at the present day, and not the Syriac Estrangelô characters made use of commonly by those who wrote in the Syriac language, and exemplified in the beautiful type in which the Syriac Gospels which he has edited are printed.

And on this ground he argues that the Greek translator manifestly mistook one Hebrew word for another, the resemblances between the two being often so close as easily to prove deceptive. Thus, in chap. i. 21, instead of "He shall save *his people*," as in the Greek, we read in this Syriac copy, "He shall save *the world*." The latter, Dr. Cureton supposes to be the genuine reading; and accounts for what he considers the error of the Greek translator, by saying, "The variation must have arisen from the similarity of לעלמא and לעמא." And so in a multitude of other cases. He supposes, continually, that the original Gospel of the Apostle having been written in the common Hebrew character, the Greek translator very often mistook, as in the instance quoted, one Hebrew word for another.

But *why the Greek translator?* Why not *the Syriac transcriber?* Admitting the soundness of Dr. Cureton's hypothesis, that the character above exemplified was that employed by St. Matthew, on what ground does he charge the blunder, which has so often been made between one Hebrew word and another, on the Greek translator rather than the Syriac transcriber? If it be supposed that St. Matthew wrote his Gospel in square Hebrew letters, very different from those usually employed by Syriac writers, how can he be sure that the person who transferred the original Gospel into the cognate language, did not himself mistake such words as those instanced above, and thus give rise to the variations now perceptible between the Syriac copy and the Greek? This supposition is at least as probable as the other. A *translator* would have his attention more fixed than a *transcriber*. The mind of the one would be in full operation, and the work in which he was engaged would of necessity be slowly executed; while the other had little more than a mechanical process to accomplish, and might very hastily, and therefore at times erroneously, perform his task. On the ground, then, which Dr. Cureton himself assumes, it is at least as probable, that the errors of the kind referred to were committed by the Syriac transcriber, as that they are to be traced to the Greek translator; and the question between them is thus shifted to the further ground,—On which side do the variations bear the appearance of mistake, and on which may there be discovered the stamp of originality and correctness?

Now, after a careful comparison of the Greek text with this Syriac copy, we can only express our amazement, that any one should hesitate as to the answer to be given to these questions. To our mind, the errors of the Syriac are so frequent and obvious, that nothing but a blinding partiality for the work which he has edited, could have prevented Dr. Cureton from discovering them. By its additions, omissions, and manifest mistranslations, this Syriac fragment of St. Matthew may be shown to be comparatively worthless, even for the humblest purposes of sacred criticism, and to be made absolutely ridiculous when it is gravely proposed as a rival of our existing Greek Gospel. We shall bring forward a few specimens of its peculiarities under each of the heads mentioned; and are quite sure that very little will be requisite, in order to expose the utter hollowness of its pretensions, as approaching more nearly than any other to the original text of the Apostle.

*First*, let us look at its *additions*. These are very frequent,—so numerous, indeed, that *amplification* may, in general, be said to be the characteristic of this Syriac copy as compared with the Greek. Now, this is in itself a very suspicious circumstance. There is no sounder rule in Biblical criticism, than that which is announced in the first of the Canons of Griesbach:—"*Brevior lectio*, nisi testium vetustorum et gravium auctoritate penitus destituatur, *præferenda est verbosiori*. Librarii enim multo proniores ad addendum fuerunt, quam ad omittendum. Consulto vix unquam prætermiserunt quicquam, addiderunt quam plurima: casu vero nonnulla quidem exciderunt, sed haud pauca etiam oculorum, aurium, memoriæ, phantasiæ ac judicii errore a scribis admisso, adjecta sunt textui." Very many passages might be quoted, in which this Syriac copy contains additions to the Greek: let the following suffice.

In the very first chapter we see the tendency displayed, by the insertion of *the three kings*, at ver. 8. There is not the slightest authority of an external kind for this addition; and it is in direct opposition to the statement made by the Evangelist himself at ver. 17. St. Matthew tells us (even in this Syriac copy), that "from David until the carrying away into Babylon, are *fourteen* generations," whereas if these three additional names be inserted, there are *seventeen;* and thus the sacred writer is made to contradict himself! In ii. 20, "to take it away" is added: in iii. 17, we read, "thou art my son and my beloved:" in iv. 24, is added, "and upon each one of them he was laying his hand:" in v. 18, we find "one letter Yod," where there is simply "one iota" in the Greek: in vi. 30, "is gathered and" is inserted; and so on, several examples of addition to the Greek usually occurring in every chapter. And it is to be observed, that many of these additions are taken from the parallel passages in the other Gospels. Thus, at v. 12, we read in the Syriac, but not in the Greek, "in that day," words which are found in the parallel passage Luke vi. 23. And so at xxi. 13, "for all nations" is inserted, in accordance with the parallel passages Mark xi. 17, and Luke xix. 46. Now, a special caution is given by Griesbach against accepting such additions as genuine. Among other reasons which should lead us specially to prefer the shorter reading, he mentions this one,—"si plenior lectio parallelis locis ad verbum consonet," which is the case with not a few of the additions to the Greek contained in this Syriac copy. It must also be noticed, that some of these additions have the manifest appearance of being interpolations. This is plainly the case with the remarkable addition at xx. 28 (found also in the Codex Bezæ, and in some other MSS. of little authority), "But seek ye that from little things ye may become great, and not from great things may become little," etc.

*Secondly,* We may glance at the *omissions.* These are much less numerous, as compared with the Greek, than are the additions; and some of them are sanctioned by the best critical texts (such as the clause *καὶ τὸ βάπτισμα, κ. τ. λ.* chap. xx. 22, 23), so that nothing can be founded upon them. There are not a few, however, which seem to indicate carelessness on the part of the Syriac writer. Thus the words *ἐν πλοίῳ* in the Greek (xiv. 13) are unrepresented in this copy; and the omission is sanctioned by no authority whatever. This seems a clear instance of inadvertence or negligence on the side of the Syriac copyist. Other omissions again, are to be explained by the influence of the parallel passages.

Thus, at chap. iv. 2, the words "and forty nights," are left out, as in the corresponding places in Mark and Luke. A curious proof of the untrustworthy character of this Syriac text, is presented in the form in which it contains the doxology to the Lord's Prayer. It is now universally admitted by Biblical scholars, that on every principle of sound criticism, that clause must be entirely rejected. It was doubtless inserted from some of the old Liturgies, and is now omitted in every critical text. But in this Syriac copy, it appears in a form which it is next to impossible to account for, except on the ground of carelessness or caprice on the part of the transcriber. The interpolated clause is *inserted*, with the omission of the words *καὶ ἡ δύναμις* in the Greek, and reads "for thine is the kingdom and the glory, for ever and ever. Amen." But the particular case of omission in this copy, which seems to us best fitted to open the eyes of all impartial readers to its true character as a clumsy translation from the Greek, is that which occurs at chap. xii. 47. That verse is, in this Syriac recension of Dr. Cureton, *entirely omitted;* and why? Let the following statement suggest the answer. It is *also* omitted in the Vatican MS. (B), and in a few other MSS. And the reason in Greek is plain. The omission manifestly resulted from the ὁμοιοτέλευτον in ver. 46, 47. Both verses end with λαλῆσαι; and thus, as in many similar instances, the transcriber's eye deceiving him, a whole verse lying between these two words was omitted. This is universally acknowledged as the account to be given of the *lacuna* in the Greek; and is so obvious, that not the most fervent admirers of the Vatican MS. plead for rejecting this verse on the weight of its authority.[y] But what explanation shall be given of the omission of this verse in the Syriac, supposing that to be what Dr. Cureton imagines that it is? How did it come to pass that the Syriac writer failed to insert this verse if he wrote independently of the Greek? And what possible account can be given of its omission, except this very obvious and satisfactory one, that the Syriac of Cureton, so singularly preferred to our existing Greek Gospel, is itself but a version from the

[y] So evident is the mistake which has here occurred in the Cod. Vat. that Mai inserts the verse, and remarks, "Hic versiculus incaute prætermissus fuit in codice." The ὁμοιοτέλευτον *does not occur* in the Syriac or Hebrew.

Greek, and that the translator either himself fell into the same snare as the transcriber of the Vatican MS., or made use of a MS. in which the error in question had already been committed?—We may now notice,

*Thirdly*, some palpable *mistranslations* which we have observed in reading over this work and comparing it with the Greek. Perhaps no better testing-passage could be selected than the very peculiar one Matt. xi. 12. In our English version, it is given as follows: "From the days of John the Baptist until now, the kingdom of heaven suffereth violence, and the violent take it by force." Our translators have here contrived to reproduce the somewhat ambiguous phraseology of the original. They have adopted language which is usually employed in a bad sense, but which does not absolutely preclude a favourable meaning. And thus it is in the Greek. The words βιάζεται, βιασταὶ and ἁρπάζουσι are in themselves certainly fitted to suggest a bad sense. But the whole *scope* of the passage shows that such is not their meaning in this place.[z] Our Lord makes use of the strong terms which have been quoted, to denote, as forcibly as possible, that ardour, impetuosity and determination of character which are required of those who would enter into heaven. That such is his meaning cannot be doubted from a consideration of the context, and is admitted by all the best critics. The opposite view which would attribute to βιάζεται the significance of "violently resisting," and ascribe it to the Pharisees, "bears," says Alford, "no sense as connected with the discourse before us." And yet this *is* the meaning assigned to the passage in the Syriac of Cureton. A word is employed, quite different from that adopted in the Peschito, and which never (in its substantive form) bears a good sense. Accordingly Dr. Cureton translates the verse as follows, to the complete subversion of those claims put forth for his work as representing the Apostolic original, or even as being a tolerably correct translation of it: "From John the Baptist's days and until now, the kingdom of heaven is *oppressed*, and its *oppressors* seize upon it." Numerous additional instances of mistranslation

[z] That βιάζομαι was sometimes used by Hellenistic writers in a good sense, appears from Gen. xxxiii. 11, where we read of Jacob in reference to Esau, καὶ ἐβιάσατο αὐτόν· "he *constrained* him."

might be brought forward: they may be found in almost every chapter; and some of them involve blunders as gross as any that could be committed by a schoolboy. Of this nature is the rendering of δικαιοσύνη, (v. 6), by a word meaning "justice," which deprives the beatitude of all meaning. It would truly be a strange and ominous benediction to pronounce on sinful men, and might even seem to carry in it a biting sarcasm, had our Lord really said, as this Syriac copy represents him, "Blessed are they who hunger and thirst for *justice*, because they shall be satisfied." Of the same description are the renderings, "against whom adultery hath not been *spoken*," (v. 32, παρεκτὸς λόγου πορνείας); "*what* is the mote thou seest," (vii. 3, τί δὲ βλέπεις τὸ κάρφος); "do not trouble me," (xx. 13, οὐκ ἀδικῶ σε) etc.

We may also notice those intensive forms which occur both in this Syriac copy and the Peschito, and which are thought by Dr. Cureton to give some countenance to the pretensions he puts forth for his edition. The following observations which he makes upon a passage of this kind, will show the nature of his reasoning, and also the length to which he is inclined to carry his theory with respect to all the first three Gospels. At chap. xx. 41, we find the rendering, "*evilly, evilly, will he destroy them,*" and the following remarks of Dr. Cureton;—"The intensitive form of ביש ביש repeated; the translator (into Greek,) does not seem to have been familiar with this, and therefore has rendered κακοὺς κακῶς ἀπολέσει αὐτούς, and the Latin *malos male perdet*. The Peschito retains the idiomatic expression as here. Both Mark and Luke have substituted for ביש ביש, *evilly, evilly*, ἐλεύσεται, probably from some defect in the original MS., almost as if there had been read in Hebrew בוא יבוא."

Now, not to mention the somewhat important fact, which Dr. Cureton entirely overlooks, that St. Matthew here reports the words of the *bystanders*, while St. Mark and St. Luke give the words of *Christ himself*, it is admitted by almost every critic that the Peschito of Matthew, like the other books, is a translation from the Greek. Even Dr. Tregelles contends for this, and on the very best grounds.[a] It follows then, of course, that the

[a] Horne and Tregelles, p. 266.

intensive form, here employed in the Syriac, is a translation from the Greek, and not *vice versa*, as Dr. Cureton argues, so that if there is an error, it falls to the side of the Syriac and not the Greek.

Further, it must be observed that, where there is not gross inaccuracy, *coarseness* is the characteristic of this Syriac copy as compared with the Greek. There is an utter want of those delicate shades of meaning which appear in our canonical Gospel (*e.g.* iii. 14): tenses and conjunctions seem at times to have been chosen very much at random; and the whole work bears unmistakeable traces of carelessness or incompetency, or both, on the part of him who produced it.

Such being the real character of this Syriac *version* (for we may now give it its right name), one feels greatly inclined to turn the whole pretensions put forth for it into ridicule. When we read in the preface of Dr. Cureton (p. xciii), that he is "fully satisfied that this Syriac text of the Gospel of St. Matthew has, to a great extent, retained the identical terms and expressions which the Apostle himself employed: and that we have here in our Lord's discourses, to a great extent the very same words as the Divine Author of our holy religion himself uttered, in proclaiming the glad tidings of salvation in the Hebrew dialect to those who were listening to him, and through them to all the world"—the query naturally occurs, "Quid dignum tanto feret hic promissor hiatu?" and when we compare the reality with the profession, it is with some difficulty that we repress the words of Horace, which immediately follow those that have been quoted. Respect for the Editor of these Remains is all that can prevent them from being made, as now put forth to the world, the object of unmeasured contempt. Never probably was there in the whole history of critical publications such a notable example of self-delusion as that under which Dr. Cureton has laboured in this undertaking. Were that all, however, little need be said upon the subject. The learned Canon has undoubtedly, by his former services to sacred study, earned the right to indulge, without rebuke, in any harmless though baseless speculations which may commend themselves to his attention. But, as will appear in the following chapter, his recent speculations have been very far from harmless. They tend naturally and of necessity to imperil the most sacred and momentous interests. They have already, to some extent, effected mischief, and, if left unchallenged to produce their proper results, they must speedily accomplish more. But happily, the claims put forth in behalf of the work in question, are seen on the slightest inspection of it to be so utterly groundless, that any evil influence which it may exert will be but limited and transient; and the work itself will soon be prized simply for the beauty of its typography—will be referred to merely as an example of that Royal patronage which is in this country extended to sacred learning, and will exist only as a memorial of the follies into which even the learned may occasionally be betrayed.

## CHAPTER V.

### RESULTS OF THE PRECEDING INQUIRY.

In this chapter we propose briefly to consider the practical results of those conclusions which have been reached in the course of the preceding Inquiry, and to compare them with the consequences that follow from the adoption of any of the other theories which have been mentioned. We have purposely abstained from referring to such results in the progress of our previous investigation, lest it should have been thought an appeal was made to any thing else than the critical judgment of the reader. But now that our inquiry has been finished, and the grounds on which our opinions rest, set on their own proper merits before the world, it seems not only right in itself, but necessary almost to the completeness of the argument, that we should glance, in this closing chapter, at the practical effects which follow from the adoption of one or other of the various theories that have been considered.

It will have been observed that nothing has been said, in the preceding chapters, respecting that *third* hypothesis which was mentioned at the beginning of this treatise as having been embraced by not a few respectable authorities—to the effect that St. Matthew wrote *both* in Greek and Hebrew, so that although it be admitted that the Hebrew original has perished, we still possess the Greek Gospel which flowed from his pen. The reason why this hypothesis has not hitherto been noticed is simply this, that as long as we were dealing with *evidence*, there was really no opportunity for bringing it under consideration. Evidence it has none. Not the least *distinctive* proof belongs to the middle hypothesis. It is avowedly a compromise between two antagonist opinions, and it leans upon both for support. Whatever plausibility or seeming evidence it possesses, is derived from borrowing both right and left (if we may be allowed the expression),—both from the hypothesis of a Greek, and from that of a Hebrew original. And accordingly we find that the supporters of this third opinion, state in the strongest terms the evidence both for the first and second. This is strikingly observable, for instance, in Olshausen among German critics, and in Lee of Dublin in this country. Olshausen says, that "while all the fathers of the church relate that Matthew wrote in Hebrew, yet they universally make use of the *Greek* text as a genuine Apostolic composition," and adds, that "our Greek Matthew is of a character so peculiar, that one cannot believe it to be a mere translation." Dr. Lee quotes these statements with approbation, and while admitting the validity of the tradition that St. Matthew wrote in Hebrew, contends very earnestly that our present Greek Gospel is also the original work of the Apostle. "All versions," he says, "even the ancient Syriac (in which dialect, be it observed, the Gospel is said to have been originally written), are taken from the present Greek of St. Matthew, and not from an unknown Aramaic original;" and he adds, that "since the concurrent voice of antiquity declares the first of our four Gospels to have proceeded from St. Matthew, we are justified in assuming that it actually *has* proceeded *in its present form* from the pen of the Apostle."[b]

Thus, unable to decide between two conflicting claims, both of which seem to them irresistible, the defenders of the third hypothesis take up a mid-way position,—a position which appears to us entirely arbitrary and indefensible, but which, like other compromises, possesses no little attraction for a certain class of minds. It seems to furnish a means of escape from all difficulties, and to reconcile all interests. The wide-spread tradition in the ancient church as to the language in which St. Matthew wrote, is fully honoured, and at the same time, the authority of our existing Gospel is preserved entire. It is not to be wondered at, therefore, that this opinion has found several ingenious advocates, and is in considerable estimation at the present day. But, notwithstanding its apparent advantages, it is, after all, only a confession of weakness. It amounts to a virtual acknowledgement on the part of those who adopt it, that they cannot decide between the mutually hostile arguments adduced in support of the first

[b] Lee on Inspiration, Appendix P.

and second hypotheses. They do, in fact, own the truth of both classes of arguments, yet they fully yield to the force of neither. And this is a very unsatisfactory state in which to rest. In any science whatever, which depends on probable evidence, a similar expedient might be adopted for getting rid of all difficult and perplexing questions. But nothing can in this way be settled. For, it is evidence only which *can* settle any question, and of evidence for this third opinion respecting St. Matthew's Gospel, there is, as has been said, none to be found. It is a mere device for evading difficulties, and therefore, we heartily concur in those terms of condemnation in which it has been spoken of both by the defenders of the Greek and Hebrew original. On the part of the former, Credner describes it as "entirely destitute of any historical foundation,"[c] and De Wette says of it, that it is "utterly baseless;"[d] while, on the part of the latter, Principal Campbell declares, with his usual vigorous sense, that it is "an opinion every way improbable, and so manifestly calculated to serve a turn, as cannot recommend it to a judicious and impartial critic."[e]

Besides these general objections which may be made to the reconciling hypothesis, there are other special grounds on which it may justly be pronounced untenable. These have been stated by Greswell in the following terms:—"The hypothesis," he says, "of a double Gospel by St. Matthew, one in Hebrew, and another in Greek; or of a double publication of the same Gospel, once in Hebrew and again in Greek; which has been invented as calculated to meet every difficulty—to save the credit of testimony, which is exclusively in favour of an Hebrew Gospel, and yet to account for the origin of the Greek, which must have superseded it, is far from producing these effects. It is clearly gratuitous; for testimony gives it no countenance whatever; besides which, it supposes what is even more improbable than an original Gospel in Greek.[f] If both these Gospels were equally intended for Jews, it seems inconceivable that the same work, designed for the same

[c] "Diese jeder geschichtlichen Grundlage eutbehrende Vermuthung."

[d] "Aus der Luft gegriffen."

[e] Preface to St. Matthew's Gospel, § 11.

[f] We would say here, "what is *almost* as improbable as an original Gospel in *Hebrew only*."

persons, should have been composed in two different languages, or translated from one language into another. The hypothesis, I believe, does not assume the publication of two such Gospels at once, but at different times; which is only to increase the difficulty. For, if St. Matthew had already published an Hebrew Gospel, it must have been because an Hebrew Gospel was sufficient; and if so, there could be no necessity for another in Greek.[g] Those who would have required a Greek Gospel, could not have wanted an Hebrew; and those who required one in Hebrew, could not have wanted one in Greek. In any case, no more than a single Gospel, and in a single language was to be expected for the benefit of the same church. Besides which, they who would have required a Greek Gospel, would have required also such explanations as even St. Matthew's Gospel has no where given; and they who would have required no such explanations, would not have required a Gospel in Greek. . . . A Greek Gospel, would be requisite for those only to whom an Hebrew Gospel would have been useless; and these we may take it for granted, would be none but the Gentiles as such: in which case it is morally certain that St. Matthew's Greek Gospel, whether an original or a translation from the Hebrew by the author of it himself, would have borne as indubitable marks of the description of readers for which it was intended, as either St. Mark's, or St. Luke's, or St. John's does."[h]

These remarks appear to us decisive of the fate of the third hypothesis, if indeed it deserves such an elaborate refutation. The mere fact that it has *no evidence* ought to be sufficient to condemn it. It was only in very recent times that it was thought of as a means of evading the difficulties of the question. The fathers, while, as we have seen, deluded into the notion of regarding the Greek Gospel as a translation, never dreamt of attributing it to the Apostle himself. Various other names were suggested

[g] True, but let our readers note the consequence. If the supposed Hebrew Gospel was *sufficient*, what need was there, as Papias tells us, for "every one" labouring to interpret it "as well as he could?" Thus do the advocates of the Hebrew original, while blindly accepting one of the statements of their principal witness, find it necessary flatly to contradict the other.

[h] Harmony of the Gospels, § i. 142.

as that of the probable translator, such as those of St. John, St. James, and even St. Paul, but never that of St. Matthew. The truth is, that if our existing Gospel be a version from the Hebrew, we know nothing whatever of the person who translated it.

The real and only choice, therefore, lies between the first and second hypotheses. We must believe either *first*, that St. Matthew wrote originally in Hebrew, and that we now possess only a version of his work, executed by some unknown translator, or *secondly*, that he wrote in Greek only, and that we still have his work as authentic and entire, as are any of the other Gospels. Many attempts have been made by the advocates of the first hypothesis, to show that although, on their supposition, our present Greek Gospel is the work of an unknown translator, we may yet accord to it the reverence which is due to inspired Scripture. Dr. Tregelles especially, has laboured to maintain this position. He says in one place (and often repeats the idea)—"Why should the fact of a book being *translated* by an *unknown* hand detract from its authority? Were not many canonical books *written* by unknown persons? Who shall say positively who *wrote* many of the Old Testament books? Who wrote Joshua, Judges, 2 Samuel, Kings, Esther, and other books? And yet God has preserved to us these inspired anonymous volumes."

But the weakness of this reasoning is only too evident. There *are*, no doubt, in the Old Testament Scriptures, some books, the authors of which we, at the present day, cannot positively determine, that nevertheless stand on precisely the same footing as the rest of the inspired volume. But Dr. Tregelles forgets to what these owe their authority. Not to mention other reasons, there is especially this one, that they were all contained in those *Scriptures*, to which our Lord himself so often gave the weight of his divine sanction and approval. Had we any thing like this for the supposed translation of St. Matthew, we should not say another word about its anonymous character. But it is needless to remark that nothing approaching to such sanction can be pleaded on its behalf. It rises in obscurity—no one knows when or where—it presents no credentials of its accuracy or fidelity, and it offers not a vestige of proof that it has any claim to be regarded as a portion of the inspired Word of God. It is vain to tell us that the fathers treated it as inspired Scripture, while asserting it to be a translation, and professing themselves ignorant of its author. Unless they give us *good and sufficient reasons* for adopting such a course, it does not follow that what satisfied them, must also satisfy us. But we do not believe that our present Greek Gospel thus lightly attained to its place in the Canon. Nothing, we are convinced, except its Apostolic origin, will account for the universal deference with which from the earliest ages it has been regarded. It was accepted by the primitive church as St. Matthew's Gospel, because it *really was so*, and as such inspired; and when, afterwards, the notion spread that the Greek was merely a translation, this error could not deprive the Gospel of that position of authority which it had already attained; and the fathers, overlooking the logical consequences of that opinion, which, after all, the most trustworthy among them only hesitatingly expressed, continued to quote and refer to it as the infallible Word of God.[1]

But let us look a little more closely at the ground occupied by those modern critics who hold that our existing Greek Gospel is merely a version from the Hebrew formed by an unknown translator, and yet claim for it the respect due to the word of Inspiration. Dr. Tregelles very properly quotes Jerome's famous

[1] The following remarks of Olshausen in support of the third hypothesis do, in reality, serve to confirm our position that St. Matthew wrote in *Greek only*. "It is a singular circumstance," he says, "that while all the fathers of the church declare Matthew to have written in Hebrew, they all, notwithstanding, make use of the Greek text as of genuine Apostolic origin, without remarking what relation the Hebrew Matthew bore to our Greek Gospel: for *that the oldest fathers of the church did not possess Matthew's Gospel in any other form than that in which we now have it is fully settled*. . . . The idea that some unknown individual translated the Hebrew Gospel of Matthew, and that this translation is our Canonical Gospel is at once contradicted by the circumstance of the universal diffusion of this same Greek Gospel of Matthew, which makes it absolutely necessary to suppose that the translation was executed by some one of acknowledged influence in the church, indeed of Apostolic authority." Olshausen, i. 28 (Clark's Foreign Theol. Library, vol. v.) It is here justly argued that nothing except the Apostolic origin of our Greek Gospel will account for the early and universal acceptance given it; but as we have not the slightest evidence that it was *translated* by Matthew or any other of the Apostles, we are bound to hold its true and exclusive originality in the form in which we still possess it.

saying, "Quis in Græcum transtulerit non satis certum est," to show how groundless are the assertions of those who maintain, that either St. Matthew himself, or some other of the Apostles, was the translator; but he does not feel how ominous is the sound of these words, as respects the authority which he claims for our existing Gospel. Is a translation, no one knows by whom (and so far as appears no one has *ever* known), to be set side by side with inspired Scripture? Who, that has any proper notion of what inspiration implies, can bear such an idea for a single moment? If inspiration is a reality at all, it distinguishes the books which possess it from all others in the world. We are not, indeed, able to show this by an exhibition of the manner in which the Spirit of God operates upon the minds of the inspired. But the works thus produced must, unless the idea of inspiration be a mere deception, be totally different in point of authority from all others, inasmuch as they, and none else, possess the attribute of infallibility, and claim to be received, without exception or qualification, as the unerring dictates of the living God.

Inspiration, then, is a very solemn peculiarity to attribute to any writing, and must not, except on the very best grounds, be either supposed or admitted. It completely isolates those books, to which it belongs, from all others, however excellent or admirable these may be reckoned. And it is highly important, at the present day carefully to preserve the vital distinction which thus exists between inspired and non-inspired books, since it is not uncommon to find, in our popular literature, a sort of inspiration spoken of as pertaining to mere human compositions. This error must be all the more guarded against, because, like every other that has obtained much currency, it involves a kind of half-truth. There *is* a sense, we readily admit, in which it may be said that the Spirit of God is the Author of *all* intellectual eminence; so that whatever is excellent or noble in any created being is to be traced to his gracious and effectual working. To Him is due every triumph of human genius, and to Him should the glory of all that intellectual power which man displays be ascribed. When the astronomer calculates, years beforehand, the courses and positions of the stars of heaven—when the metaphysician draws his fine distinctions, and grapples successfully with that very mind which serves him—when the poet's eye, rolling in ecstasy, contemplates the gorgeous visions which flit before his imagination, and when he seizes and incarnates these in words for the delight and admiration of mankind—when the historian gives life, and interest, and value to the deeds of bygone ages by the graphic style and the philosophic spirit in which he narrates them—when, in short, any proof whatever is presented of the exercise of mental superiority, there do we gladly acknowledge the working of the Spirit of God—of Him who at first made man "a living soul," who filled the heart of the skilful Bezaleel with wisdom, and understanding, and knowledge, and who is still promised as a Spirit of counsel and of might to all them that ask Him.

But, while we readily admit these truths, we must guard against the erroneous inference which some have drawn from them,—that the inspiration claimed by and for the writers of Scripture, is the same in kind with that which is enjoyed by the possessors of natural genius. Not a few will acknowledge at once the inspiration of David, Isaiah, and Paul; but it is just in the same sense as they maintain that of Homer, or Plato, or Milton. Now, this is a pernicious confounding of things which are, in reality, entirely different. There is, as every sincere believer in Scripture must feel, an essential difference indicated in the Bible itself, between the nature of that influence which is exerted upon the mind of the secular poet or historian, and that which goes forth upon the sacred Prophet or Evangelist,—a difference so vast, that it is an utter abuse of language to call the two things by the same name. It may be, for aught we can tell, that the process by which the Spirit operates upon the mind is as simple in the one case as the other. The *modus operandi* is equally unknown to us, with respect to the sacred as to the secular writer. But while we can say nothing about the differences which may exist as to the *manner* in which the Divine power is applied, we know to a certainty, that there is an infinite difference in the *results* which are produced. *This* grand peculiarity belongs to every inspired book (*πᾶσα γραφὴ θεόπνευστος*, every God-breathed writing), that it is *absolutely and unerringly true*, and may thus be taken by man as a sure and infallible guide. If this attribute be denied to the books of Scripture, we are only playing with words while we continue to talk of their inspiration; and if this attribute be admitted, they are elevated to a height where they exist alone: they differ, essentially and entirely, from every other book, however excellent or able, which has ever been presented to the world.

We have been led to make these remarks in connexion with the position occupied by Dr. Tregelles, as regards the existing Gospel of St. Matthew. He maintains, that our Greek Gospel is a version by some unknown person, of the original work of the Apostle, and yet claims for it the same respect and submission that we yield to the rest of Scripture. Now, for our own part, we can never consent, that the solemn, the peculiar, the almost *awful* attribute of inspiration, should be ascribed to any work on such grounds. Our very reverence for inspired Scripture requires that we should be cautious, yea, most scrupulous, in acknowledging the claims of any work to be so regarded. We are thankful, that the Bible comes to us so manifestly bearing the impress of its heavenly origin, and at the same time so abundantly supported by external evidence. But, if driven to believe, as Dr. Tregelles does, that one of its books is simply a translation of an originally inspired work;—a translation made, no one knows by whom, and possessing, so far as we can learn, no Apostolic authority; a translation, moreover, which bears in itself unmistakeable evidence, that the translator *tampered* with the copy before him, our confidence is at once shaken, not only in that particular book, but also, to some extent, in the whole professedly inspired volume, of which it forms a part.

Dr. Tregelles says as little as possible, with respect to the relation subsisting between what he deems our present Greek translation of St. Matthew, and the Apostle's original work. But every candid inquirer must perceive, that, on his supposition, the translator has taken no small liberties with the original. We have seen that this is the case with regard to the manner in which citations are made from the Old Testament; and it also appears in other particulars, as most of the defenders of the Hebrew original have confessed. Dr. Davidson plainly declares, that "any conclusion to which a modern writer comes in regard to changes or additions made by the translator, depends largely on subjective feeling. *It rests on the doctrinal position he has previously taken.*"[k] It is plain, that room is thus left for discarding as much of the Gospel as any one pleases, while, at the same time, he could not, on the hypothesis of the Hebrew original, be charged with the impiety of setting aside the Word of Gôd, since he might plead, that the passages he rejected had been added by the translator, and as such deserved no reverence. Dr. Davidson admits (as, indeed, every one holding the Hebrew original must admit, in order to escape absurdity), that the numerous explanations of words and customs which occur in our Greek Gospel, were inserted by the translator. And if these, why not more? How can we be sure that *any* of the passages peculiar to St. Matthew really had a place in the original work, and were not inserted by the translator? How can we know with certainty, that the closing words of the Gospel,—words, in several points of view, so important,—really ever issued from the Saviour's lips? And so with everything else in the first Gospel, that is unconfirmed by any of the others. In all such cases, we are completely at the mercy of the translator,—a translator of whose faithfulness we have no guarantee, but of whose temerity in changing, and adding to, his original, we have indubitable evidence,—a translator of whom no one, ancient or modern, ever heard; whose name was never whispered even in the very age when his work is supposed to have been issued, and of whose qualifications, no less than of his very existence, a profound silence is maintained by all antiquity.

It is manifest, then, that Dr. Tregelles' position, as the advocate at once of the Hebrew original and of the plenary inspiration of our first Gospel, is utterly inconsistent and untenable. The *real* result to which the hypothesis of a Hebrew original leads has been brought out in its plain colours by several other writers. Some of these certainly evince a far less reverent spirit than Dr. Tregelles, but they reason far more logically on the premises with which he furnishes them. Thus, it was long ago said by Michaelis, "If we have really lost the original work of St. Matthew, and possess nothing except a Greek translation, we certainly can

[k] Introduction, i. 47.

ascribe to the words no such thing as inspiration: it is even possible that here and there the true meaning of the Apostle has been mistaken by the translator."[l] To the same effect, Jones (a writer of a very different school from Michaelis) expresses himself as follows, with regard to the hypothesis that our existing Gospel is a version from the Hebrew: "For all we know to the contrary, it may be a very false and corrupt translation; it may be done by a person no way qualified for such a work: and does not this now make its authority dubious and uncertain? For my part, I freely own if I believed it to be a translation made by a person I know nothing of, I could not yield it that same respect, and have that same value for it, as the other parts of the sacred writings."[m]

But not only must the existing Gospel of Matthew be abandoned if the hypothesis of its Hebrew original be maintained, the whole New Testament canon is also unsettled, and our confidence in its authority to some extent lessened. For, on what ground do we accept it as inspired Scripture? Simply because the early church did so, and because we believe that the greatest pains were taken by the primitive Christians to have certain evidence of the Apostolic origin of every book before it was admitted into the canon. But what shall be said of their manner of acting with respect to the Greek Gospel of St. Matthew, if that be regarded as a translation? Here we have a book referred to as inspired Scripture, and elevated to the pre-eminent position which, as we have seen, is involved in such a distinction, while no trouble seems to have been taken to discover on what ground its authority rested; and no one appears to have known through whose hands it passed in exchanging its original Apostolic form for that in which we now possess it. It is certain that the early Christians who adopted the notion of its being a version from the Hebrew, were as much in the dark respecting the translator as we are. Jerome's well-known words on this point have already been quoted; and if, with all the uncertainty which he says attached to the vital

[l] "Haben wir von Matthäo den Grundtext verloren, und nichts als eine griechische Uebersetzung: so können wir freilich den Worten keine göttllche Eingebung zuschreiben: ja es ist möglich, dass an ein und anderm Orte der wahre Sinn des Apostels von dem Uebersetzer verfehlet ist."—Einl. ii. 997.

[m] Jones on the Canon, iii. 250.

question, who translated the original work, the translation was nevertheless received as infallible Scripture, it is plain, that our confidence in the principles which guided the early church in this essential inquiry, is very much diminished. As has been previously said, *we* take a very different view of the manner in which our Greek Gospel attained to its place in the canon; but on the supposition of its being a version, it seems impossible, that our reliance on the grounds usually assigned for the authority of the New Testament generally, should not be greatly weakened. This conclusion has, in fact, been reached by some writers on the subject. These derive, from the data with which Dr. Tregelles furnishes them, several inferences from which he sensitively shrinks. Thus in a recent publication, we find an attempt made (and successfully made, if the premises be granted) to damage the whole New Testament, from the assumption made with respect to the Gospel of St. Matthew. "The theory of inspired dictation, or literary infallibility," says Dr. Donaldson, "takes account of the canonical books only, but extends itself to all of them, without reservation or exception. Consequently, the tradition, which constitutes the canon of Scripture, is the sole criterion of infallible authority; and if it is admitted that any document, though canonical, is yet of uncertain or precarious importance—(as he quite correctly argues is the case with St. Matthew's Gospel, "if the general tradition respecting it be received")—it must follow, that a place in the canon does not bestow a character of infallibility, and that the theory of inspired dictation or guidance, is not more applicable to a canonical work, than to any other ancient writings."[n]

The question, then, which has been discussed in this treatise, is one of vast importance, not only in regard to the Gospel of St. Matthew, but the whole of the New Testament Scriptures. It is, in truth, the very *Thermopylæ* of sacred criticism. On this ground the decisive battle must be fought: the fate of the whole inspired Scriptures is, to a great extent, involved in its issue; and when we take up the position occupied by Dr. Tregelles, it is

[n] "Christian Orthodoxy reconciled with the conclusions of modern Biblical learning," p. 162,—a clever, but infidel and pernicious publication.

only too plain, that the result must prove disastrous to the friends of divine revelation, and that the cause of inspired truth is irretrievably lost.

A few words may now be said respecting the practical result which follows from the views of Dr. Cureton. And that result is not far to seek: it appears, plainly and confessedly, on the very face of his publication. Of all the forms in which the hypothesis of the Hebrew original has been set forth and advocated in this country, that of Cureton, while one of the most thorough-going and consistent, is, perhaps, the one most to be regretted. Tregelles, Davidson, Greswell, and others, though earnestly maintaining the theory of the Hebrew original, yet do their best to persuade us that the existing Greek Gospel of St. Matthew, is one in which confidence may be placed. But Dr. Cureton speaks out plainly and decidedly. He sets himself elaborately to prove the mistakes which occur in our present Greek Gospel, and endeavours, with his whole might, to convince us that it is full of errors. He still, indeed, honours it with the appellation of "canonical;" but how little this word means with him, in a practical point of view, will be apparent from such a passage as the following:—"The reader will find," he says, "that, in many instances where this text and the Greek version of St. Matthew differ from each other, the variation may easily be accounted for, upon the highly probable supposition, that the translator, or the scribe who copied the MS. made use of by him, read the original Aramaic in a slightly different manner; sometimes substituting one Hebrew letter from another that closely resembled it, or confounding one similar word with another, and sometimes making omissions in consequence of the close repetition of the same word or syllable,—things which every one, who has had any experience in the collation of MSS., knows to be of very frequent occurrence; and that, upon reference to several parallel passages, in which the other Evangelists are presumed to have made use of the same original Aramaic, this text is found to agree with them, while it differs from the Greek of Matthew; and further, that if we place this Syriac text by the side of them, some slight variations in the Greek of those parallel passages themselves, can not only be explained and accounted for in the same manner, but sometimes also, upon the ground of a different Greek meaning having been given to an Aramaic particle of a twofold signification."[o]

And while Dr. Cureton thus deprives us of all confidence in our present Greek Gospel of St. Matthew (not to mention here those of St. Mark and St. Luke), he substitutes next to nothing in its place. Having taken away the full and complete Gospel which we possess, he holds out to us a *fragment* in return. And even that fragment, with all his fondness for it, he deems corrupted. "I believe," he says,[p] "that even this text is not entirely free from changes and alterations, arising from subsequent collation with the Greek, such as were afterwards carried to a much greater degree." And he proposes it as a task which remains for some "acute and judicious critic, to mark precisely those passages which have undergone the greatest change,"—a task which he himself has some hope of undertaking and accomplishing.

The work of Dr. Cureton was, no doubt, prepared and published under the influence of the most conscientious motives, yet it is difficult to find language sufficiently strong (without being offensive), in which to condemn it. He says very truly in his preface, that "on a subject of such deep weight as the Gospels, no one can be too cautious, how he propounds any theory or speculation at all varying from that which has been most generally received, even if he have almost demonstrative evidence to support the views which he takes." As produced under the influence of such feelings, and with a sincere desire to aid what is deemed the truth, this work of Dr. Cureton deserves our respect; but we must, nevertheless, be allowed strongly to express our sense of the practical mischief which it is fitted to accomplish. Coldness or hesitation in this matter would be a crime; and therefore we must plainly declare, that the consequences which follow from Dr. Cureton's theory are, in our estimation, as injurious as his theory itself was formerly shown to be baseless. Few of the German rationalists have proceeded to such an extreme, as that to

[o] Cureton's Syriac Gospels, p. xc.
[p] Id. p. xciii.

which the views of Dr. Cureton necessarily lead with respect to the Gospels. He seeks (not intentionally, but in effect,) to rob us of our dearest treasures; but, if we must part with them, it shall not, at least, be without an effort to defend them. Let truth alone be sought, and let truth prevail: but as long as we are convinced that truth ensures to us those great and holy words which are contained in our present Gospels, as "the Words of God," we must not be deterred from seeking to preserve them, by the pain of somewhat rudely dispelling a dangerous yet flattering delusion, which a fancied great discovery has fostered.[q]

It is with no feeling of boastfulness, that the reader is now asked to consider the very different result which follows from the adoption of that hypothesis which it has been the object of this treatise to establish. We have tried to show, that the Evangelist Matthew wrote his Gospel in Greek only; and that this inspired account of our Lord's actions and discourses, we at the present day possess. If this has been effected, we may be allowed to congratulate ourselves on the result. The work of St. Matthew

[q] How soon the evil to be apprehended from such a work as that of Dr. Cureton descends from the region of criticism to that of common life, will be apparent from the following remarks on it which recently appeared in one of our most widely circulated daily newspapers:—"The publication of these remarkable fragments cannot fail to give fresh force to a call for a revision of the received version of the Gospels. The reverence which shrinks from disturbing the authority of forms of words hallowed by their adoption in the church for many centuries, must yield to the conviction that the sacred cause of truth compels a closer investigation into their purity. No point of doctrine will be disturbed, no article of faith will be shaken. We have simply to admit to ourselves that the records transmitted to us of the life and teaching of our Saviour are the relations of men subject to errors like ourselves—under the influence of the Holy Spirit in respect to the doctrines they were deputed to reveal to their fellow-men; not, we may be allowed to believe, in the form and terms of their proclamation of those truths."—*Daily News*, Feb. 18, 1859.

Thus confidence is shaken, and scepticism engendered among the people, by such rash and unfounded speculations as are those of Cureton. *He* is responsible for the promulgation of the sentiments expressed by the writer just quoted. And it is earnestly to be hoped that if Dr. Cureton is, as we believe him to be, a sincere and earnest friend of sacred truth, he will be led to perceive the grievous error which he has committed; as in that case he will doubtless be ready at once to confess it, and will put forth the most strenuous efforts in order to repair the mischief which has already, to some extent, been perpetrated.

is in our hands, entire and perfect, as it proceeded from his pen, excepting only those slightly erroneous readings, which have of necessity crept into this, as into the other Gospels, with the lapse of time. These it is the object of textual criticism to correct; and these all must be strongly stimulated to remove, who believe, as we do, that in seeking after the genuine Greek expressions, we are in quest of the very words of God. Let this be believed, and criticism acquires a dignity and grandeur which cannot otherwise belong to it. Let the Biblical critic, while he pores over ancient MSS., remember that he is seeking the very words of inspiration, and he will be strengthened and encouraged in his anxious and painful toil. "*The word of the Lord*" is truly precious; and when through diligence and perseverance the sacred critic has made sure that he has found it, he may justly say with the Psalmist, "I rejoice at *thy word*, as one that findeth great spoil." But if, on the other hand, it is only *man's words*, after all, that he is in quest of, his zeal may well abate, and his efforts be suspended. Are not one man's words just as good as another's? Why, then, not rest satisfied with the Gospels as they are, instead of wearing life and strength away, in the fruitless labour of discarding one set of human words in order to adopt another,—in setting aside one Greek expression which a *transcriber* may have preferred, just to replace it by another Greek expression which a *translator* may have employed? It is evident, that, as the view which we have maintained in this treatise, is the only one which comports with the ascription of Divine authority to the existing Gospel of St. Matthew, and the only one which justifies and confirms our confidence in the remainder of the canon, so it is also the only one which imparts a meaning or value to those critical studies, which have for their object the discovery and restoration of the original text of our existing Gospels.

A *second* result has been reached in the course of the preceding investigation. In connexion with our leading subject of inquiry, we have had occasion to consider the question as to the language which our Lord usually employed, and have found reason to conclude that it was the Greek. And this, too, is a point which seems worthy of a little more particular consideration. Some writers, indeed, have spoken of this question as if it were not only destitute of practical importance, but of general interest, and could attract attention only as a matter of fruitless historical curiosity, or dry "antiquarian"[r] research. Now, we confess ourselves utterly unable to view the question in this light. It seems to us, *in itself*, and independent of all practical purposes, to be a most interesting subject of inquiry. To ascertain the language which the Son of God spoke when he dwelt upon the earth—to find out, it may be, that in our existing Gospels we have the very words which He employed, and can reproduce to ourselves the tones in which He uttered them—this appears to us a matter interesting to far more than the antiquary, and to appeal to the heart of every earnest, loving Christian. Who would not feel a new interest in the beautiful words, "Come unto me all ye that labour and are heavy laden, and I will give you rest," or the sublime words, "I am the resurrection and the life; he that believeth in me, though he were dead, yet shall he live," if he ascertained beyond a doubt that these words, as they stand in our Greek Testaments, were the very words which proceeded out of the Saviour's mouth? It may be ridiculed by some as a sentimental weakness; but, for our own part, we are not ashamed to confess that, when we read the Gospels and reflect that in these the *ipsissima verba* of the Divine Man have been recorded, the book is invested with a new interest, and we feel as if introduced within the very circle of the Saviour's hearers, who, it is said, "all bare Him witness, and wondered at the gracious words which proceeded out of His mouth."

But, in truth, everything associated with our blessed Lord rises far above any merely sentimental or antiquarian interest. Whence, for instance, that attraction which the Land of Palestine has possessed for Christians in every century of our era? Why is it that those crowds of pilgrims and travellers have flocked to it? and how comes it to pass that their tale, though a thousand times repeated, still finds eager and listening ears? Is it from the *antiquarian* curiosity which prevails with respect to the ruins of that country? Is it any motive of that kind which leads the temporary sojourner in that land to peer so anxiously into Jacob's well,

[r] This is the term employed by Dr. Fairbairn in reference to this matter. Herm. Man. chap. i. p. 2.

or to gaze so intently on the Mount of Olives? Nay: it is because the Land is so closely associated in the minds of all Christians with Him they love. It is on that account that the tourist observes with so much earnestness, and the reader listens to his tale with so great avidity. It is because *He* once trod them, that even the narrow, repulsive streets of Jerusalem have an interest which none else on earth can equal: it is because *He* once dwelt there, that the unpretending Nazareth has power to stir so deeply the hearts of its many visitors. And, if even the soil on which He trod, and the localities with which He was connected—things utterly extraneous to Himself—can thus attract and affect the Christian, shall it be said that the question respecting the language which He used—the words which He uttered—the medium He employed for laying bare to us His heart, for making us acquainted with His truest self—is one of mere antiquarian interest? Surely such is a very low and unworthy view to take of it; and although no utilitarian purpose whatever be served by the inquiry, it is still one which may well stimulate to diligence in its prosecution, and which will be felt amply to reward pains and industry in its settlement.[s]

But it may also be shown to have a practical importance. We may sometimes derive no small advantage in reading the Gospels, from noting the delicate shades of meaning which are suggested in the discourses which they contain, by the employment of different *Greek* words. Strangely enough, this has been observed and dwelt upon by some writers, who, after all, believed that our Lord and his disciples usually spoke in *Aramaic*. Thus Dean Trench remarks on Martha's saying to our Lord (John xi. 22, "But I know that even now, whatsoever thou wilt *ask* of God, God will give it thee")—"She uses the word *αἰτεῖν* (*ὅσα ἂν αἰτήσῃ*), a word never used by our Lord to express his own asking of the Father, but always *ἐρωτᾶν*; for there is a certain familiarity, nay authority, in his askings, which this word expresses, but that would not." Now there is, we believe, great propriety and force in this observation, if it be admitted that both our Lord and Martha spoke in Greek, and actually used these

[s] See an eloquent passage on this point in Diodati's *Epistola ad Lectorem.*

very expressions; but if it be supposed, as is generally done, that Aramaic was the language which He and his disciples employed, it is difficult to see on what the learned writer's remarks can rest. It will scarcely be maintained by any that precisely equivalent expressions to αἰτέω and ἐρωτάω were used in the Aramaic tongue, and that the Holy Spirit led to the choice of these Greek words in order exactly to represent the original expressions. It is scarcely possible that the fine distinction, noted by the Dean as existing between the two Greek words, should be found in exactly the same degree in any other language. The distinction is utterly lost in English, although we have many words nearly synonymous with "ask;" and, in like manner, although there may have been different terms in use in the Aramæan to express the idea of *asking*, it seems altogether unlikely that any of them should have been capable of representing the exact shade of meaning which has been noticed as distinguishing the two Greek verbs.[t] So also with regard to the distinction which the same writer notes between ἀγαπῶ and φιλῶ (John xi. 3, 5; xxi. 15–17.)[u] We can easily see a propriety, as Dr. Trench remarks, in the change of terms which occurs in these passages, provided it be granted that our Lord and his disciples *actually* made use of the words in question; but if we suppose them to have spoken in Aramaic, and these to be merely *translations* of the terms which they employed, it seems little better than learned trifling to endeavour to fix such subtle distinctions between them.

The following observations are from the pen of one well entitled to be heard on the subject. "It was," says Dr. Black,[x] "in the so called Hebrew, or popular language of the nation, that Paul addressed the multitude assembled in the streets of Jerusalem beside the castle, though they were evidently prepared to listen

[t] It is true that a different verb is used in the Peschito to translate αἰτέω in the verse here referred to from what is employed in such passages as John xiv. 26. But at John xvi. 23, we find the same Syriac verb employed to translate ἐρωτήσετε and αἰτήσητε.

[u] See Trench, *Notes on the Miracles*, p. 393 and p. 465. In the first case, the distinction noted between ἀγαπῶ and φιλῶ is preserved in the Peschito: in the second, one verb is used throughout the passage in Syriac as in English.

[x] Late Professor of Exegetical Theology in the Free Church College, Edinburgh.

to him with intelligence, when they expected him to address them in Greek. But it was in Greek that his discourses were generally spoken, and the Greek student of the New Testament, by placing himself in the position of those to whom these discourses were addressed, and realizing to himself what may still be ascertained of the very tones of the voice with which the words were uttered, will be in possession of an important exegetical principle for obtaining more vivid conceptions of the depth of meaning conveyed by the voice of the speaker." He refers in illustration of this remark to John vii. 28, where our Lord repeats the words of the people, and which, he says, "should be marked as interrogative or quasi-interrogative." But unfortunately, Dr. Black also adopts (though apparently with some reluctance) the common notion that our Lord usually spoke in Aramaic, and thus deprives himself, to a great extent of "the important exegetical principle" which he acknowledges. "The addresses of our Lord," he says, "seem from the examples given of some of the words that He spoke, to have been delivered in the common Aramæan of the age and country: but the Greek form in which they have been transmitted in the Gospels by the Evangelists who recorded them under the guidance of Inspiration, still puts it in the power of the student substantially to listen to the voice of Him who spake as never man spake." We find it somewhat difficult to form an idea of what is here meant by listening *substantially* to the voice of Christ in the Gospels, if we do not so in *reality*. In *every* faithful translation we have the substance of our Lord's words preserved. The only difference (and in some points of view, doubtless, vitally important difference,) between the Greek version of them and all others, is that in the one case the translation was made by inspired men, while, in other cases, the translators simply employed their natural powers. But this does not touch the point at present under consideration. Inspiration cannot effect impossibilities. It cannot make a *translation* of our Lord's words, to be the *very words* which He spoke. And, so far as "listening substantially" to His voice is concerned, we cannot see how the reader of His sayings in Greek, occupies any position of advantage over the reader of the same in English, unless, as we are firmly convinced, and have endeavoured to show, we do in very deed listen, in the Greek of the Evangelists, to the identical words which proceeded out of our Saviour's mouth.

How great the satisfaction of being able to believe that this is the case! How vivid and impressive the emotions awakened by the thought, that in the striking words preserved by St. Mark, *Σιώπα, πεφίμωσο*, we have the very command by which our Lord stilled the raging deep—that in the *Πάτερ ἡμῶν* of St. Matthew and St. Luke, we possess the very terms in which Christ taught his disciples to address their Father in heaven—and that in the marvellous prayer recorded in John xvii., we hear the very tones of his divine yet supplicating voice, we listen to the majestic words in which Deity on earth then called upon Deity in heaven! This then is the second result which has been reached in the course of our inquiry: Jesus spoke for the most part in Greek, and in our present Greek Gospels we still possess the very words which He employed.

A *third* conclusion, which to some may appear the most important of all, has also been attained in the preceding inquiry,—that, namely, which refers to the origin of the Gospels. It has hitherto been the *opprobrium criticorum*, that they have not been able to give any probable account of this matter. It seems now as if a sort of despair had taken the place of those violent efforts which were once put forth in this direction; although, as we have seen, every now and then, new theories (or old ones made to look new), are presented to the world. Dr. Lee expresses himself, as if he believed there was no possible means of settling the question; and while giving a sketch of the various theories which have been proposed, makes known his opinion regarding them as follows; "I am far from insinuating that the several hypotheses are on a par in point of ingenuity or of literary merit: but it can scarcely be asserted that any among them possesses much superiority over its fellows on the score of probability."[y]

Now, if we have succeeded in our argument, this vexed question may be regarded as settled. We are able to give an easy and natural account of all the phenomena presented by the Gospels. According to our hypothesis, both the coincidences and diversities observable between the Evangelists, are altogether such as were

[y] Lee on Inspiration, p. 562: see also p. 324.

to be expected. They *agree*, because they were all well acquainted with the subjects of which they treated, and because they all wrote in the same language that our Lord had spoken. They *differ*, because they were all independent writers, and naturally expressed themselves in their own individual manner and style, according to their several dispositions and acquirements.

This last proposition as to the *independence* of the first three Evangelists, may now be said to be generally admitted among our leading Biblical scholars. The evidence for it which is presented in the Gospels themselves, is such as to be felt irresistible by almost every earnest and candid mind. And thus the famous saying of Augustine, so often repeated by sacred critics, that Mark was a mere copyist and abbreviator of Matthew (pedissequus et breviator), is finally renounced as a mistake. It is found inconsistent with the internal phenomena presented by the Gospels themselves, and therefore, notwithstanding the great name of its author and the long acceptance which it met with from the critical world, it is now by general consent abandoned.

And in this, we may remark, there is found an analogous course of procedure to that which has been followed in this treatise. In both cases, *internal* evidence is allowed to decide the question at issue. The words of Jerome (or others) respecting Matthew, like those of Augustine respecting Mark, are after all but the *verba magistri* (*machtsprüche*, as the Germans say), which have been allowed to lead opinion in the church too long, but which ought, the one as well as the other, to be brought to the enduring test of the internal evidence which the Gospels themselves present. This has been done by others with respect to the saying of Augustine, and the consequence has been that its influence has now ceased to be felt: this we have endeavoured to do in the preceding pages with respect to the statements of Papias and his followers, with what effect remains to be seen.

Another observation must be made with respect to some of the theories which have been noticed in the course of our investigation. It should be borne in mind that, while, as was previously remarked, we are not at liberty to call in the inspiration of the writers of Scripture, to aid us in solving a difficulty which arises from some opinion of our own, it ought at the same time to be sufficient evidence to us of the unsoundness of any hypothesis, if it appears plainly inconsistent with the doctrine of inspiration. But, this has been greatly forgotten by those who have speculated on the subject of the origin of the Gospels. They have devised and promulgated theories which are manifestly repugnant to all notion of the inspiration of the sacred writers. And yet the books of Scripture have been received by these theorists, as, for the most part, genuine and authentic documents. Now, if there be one thing more evident than another in the New Testament, it is the claim which it puts forth to be recognised as an inspired book. And if the four Gospels are acknowledged as a genuine portion of the canon (which is granted by those critics to whom we now refer), they at once take rank with those sacred writings of which the Apostle Paul declares, "All Scripture is given by inspiration of God." Admitting then, that the Gospels are thus divinely inspired, it is utterly inconsistent to proceed to the formation of such a hypothesis respecting their origin, as plainly appears, or may easily be shown, to be repugnant to that fundamental doctrine. And let the reader only consider for a moment the various hypotheses which have been described—the original-gospel theory, and the copying theory, with the several modifications of these that have been proposed, and then say if he can believe in the inspiration of the writers, while he rests in any one of these hypotheses. If he cannot do so, he is bound to reject the doctrine of inspiration altogether, or rather, and infinitely better, reject the false and delusive theory which is proved inconsistent with it. Reason demands that either the inspiration of the sacred writers, or the theories opposed to it, which have been invented by their critics, should be abandoned. Rejecting their inspiration, one is free to form any hypothesis with respect to the origin of their works which ingenuïty can devise, and which common sense will tolerate.[1] But, admitting their inspiration, the account which is

[1] But even *common sense* rebels against the complicated theories which have been devised on this subject. It expresses itself in the following remarks of Schleiermacher. "For my part," he says, "I find it quite enough to prevent me from conceiving the origin of our first three Gospels according to Eichhorn's theory, that I am to figure to myself our good Evangelists surrounded by five or six open rolls or books, and that too in different languages,

given of their works must be consistent with that fact. Either *rationalism* in its most imperious and haughty form, disdaining to take into consideration the idea of their heavenly origin in dealing with the phenomena which they present, must be allowed the fullest scope; or *reverence*, which gratefully acknowledges them as divine, must restrict itself to such an account of their special features and characteristics, as will be in harmony with that great fundamental principle.

And can any of our readers hesitate as to which of these alternatives should be chosen? Shall we, from a blind reverence for some statements of antiquity—statements which can be proved absurd and contradictory—allow ourselves to be robbed of those blessed words of truth and consolation, by which alone the present life is rendered happy and hopeful, and by which alone there is a gleam of brightest sunshine cast upon the dark hereafter? Are any so wedded to ancient opinions and to human theories, as that they will cling to these, though they should have to let the Bible go altogether, or at least to resign its claims as the sure and infallible Word of God? Why should agreement with antiquity be purchased at such a price? What should prevent us from looking with our own eyes at the Gospels, and drawing our own inferences from the phenomena which they present? This is what we have ventured to do in the preceding pages; and although we have

looking by turns from one into another, and writing a compilation from them. I fancy myself in a German study of the eighteenth or nineteenth century, rather than in the primitive age of Christianity, and if this resemblance diminishes perhaps my surprise at the well known image having suggested itself to the critic in the construction of his hypothesis, it renders it the less possible for me to believe that such was the actual state of the case."—*The Gospel of St. Luke*, (p. 6, quoted by Lee on Inspiration, p. 324). Schleiermacher's own theory will be found described in Horne's Introd., vol. iv. p. 653, and is quite as unsatisfactory as any that preceded it. Considering the complicated and contradictory hypotheses which have been framed on this subject by continental critics, one scarcely wonders to find another great German, Goethe—expressing himself in the following terms respecting the Gospels: "Es ist ein Meer auszutrinken, wenn man sich in eine historische und critische Untersuchung dieserhalb einlässt. Man thut immer besser, sich ohne Weiteres an das zu halten, was wirklich da ist, und sich davon auzueignen, was man für seine sittliche Cultur und Stärkung gebrauchen kann." Eckermann's Gespräche mit Goethe, ii. 265.

thus reached some conclusions opposed to the opinions of ancient writers, we are not on that account to be held as discrediting their testimony or disparaging their judgment. On many grounds they deserve our veneration; but when they make statements which appear inconsistent with truth, they certainly ought not to be followed; and however long the false opinion may have reigned, it is to be unceremoniously rejected: for, as one of the fathers themselves excellently observes, "custom, without truth, is only the old age of error."[a]

We have tried then to show that there is a simple theory suggested by the Gospels themselves with respect to their origin, which explains all fancied difficulties and accounts for all actual facts. And whether we have succeeded or not in establishing our theory, there is manifest need that *some hypothesis or other* should be devised which will still leave us in possession of an inspired revelation from heaven. As a large experience has proved, the world cannot do without the Bible. Not the greatest advances in civilization—not the mightiest efforts of human genius, will make up for the want of that heaven-inspired volume. God's words are like the stars of the firmament; they are abiding and unerring, so that they may safely be trusted to for direction: man's words, again, when compared with these, are, even at the highest, but like brilliant meteors, which may for a moment dazzle the eye, but which can furnish no steady or trustworthy guidance to the anxious traveller to eternity.

In order to be convinced of the infinite preciousness of the Bible, we have only to remember what the world was without that book-revelation which it is the fashion of some in our own day to despise, and what it still remains in those lands where that volume is as yet unknown. As if to test human ability to the utmost, it was long ere the ancient Scriptures found their way beyond the narrow province of Judæa; and it has been but slowly that the book which contains the full revelation of God's character and will has advanced throughout the earth. Men were left for ages to exert their powers in devising a substitute for a direct revelation from heaven,—and what was the result? Let the state

[a] "Consuetudo, sine veritate, vetustas erroris est."—Cyprian.

of the heathen world at the birth of Christ return an answer. There was then no fixed system of morals, but vice was mistaken for virtue, and good was confounded with evil; there were no true ideas of God,—but the ignorant were worshippers of *many*, and the learned scarcely of *any* deities: there were no just views of the nature and destiny of man,—but while some dreamt of immortality, others openly denied it: superstition—vile and debasing, or atheism—void and cheerless, were the only alternatives presented to man's choice; and either of these led to the extinction of all that was noblest in his nature, and to a complete disregard of morality and virtue. In ancient Greece, refined yet superstitious—in ancient Rome, civilized yet sunk in wickedness—in ancient Britain, both rude and immoral, we see what our world was without the Bible: and in modern China, Hindostan, and Turkey,—the countries now most favourably representative of the extra-Christian world, we see what, without that book, it would have remained until this day. To the Bible the world is indebted for all that it knows of the true character both of God and man, and of the relations subsisting between them; from its sacred pages have been drawn all the most ennobling sentiments and all the pious maxims which pervade and enrich the literature of our day: and but for it the earth in which we live would still have been the dark abode of ignorance and vice, filled with beings who knew no God save the product of their own evil hearts, and who owned no laws but such as their own corrupt minds devised. From it has gone forth the power which has changed our own country from the condition of barbarism and wretchedness in which it once lay into that state of civilization and comfort in which we now behold it. And what the Bible has done for Britain, the Bible can do for every nation under heaven. It needs but the free circulation and the universal study of that book to reclaim men everywhere from the bondage of vice and superstition; and it needs but the practice of its humanizing maxims, and the copying of its one perfect example, in order to chase away savage manners from the earth; to break the power of selfishness and ambition; to banish war and its horrible accompaniments; to extirpate vice, and tyranny, and oppression, in all those hideous forms in which they so often present themselves; to constitute mankind one great and loving brotherhood; and to knit all human hearts together in the blessed bonds of unity and peace.

Such, then, as experience proves, being the preciousness of the Bible to the world at large, it is the cause of humanity which we defend, when we seek to uphold its authority. This we have humbly endeavoured to do in this treatise, in opposition to some other theories, which have plainly a contrary tendency. And whether successful or not in our attempt, it is at least a gratifying conviction which we cherish, that the views we have propounded cannot prove injurious to those momentous interests it has been our purpose to advance. No hypothesis has been started by us, which is fitted to imperil or destroy the influence of that book which is the source of every Christian's hopes. We have tried to bear in mind throughout this discussion, its peculiarly sacred character. And that should surely be done by all the professed friends of the Bible, in whatever speculations they may engage with respect to any portion of its contents. If accepted at all, it should be accepted for what it professes to be—an inspired revelation of the mind and will of God. And while truth is earnestly sought in every point connected with it,—while no trembling solicitude about *consequences* deters us from the most rigorous application of sound critical principles, and the honest declaration of the results to which they lead, let it nevertheless be remembered, that the book with which we deal is a professedly inspired volume, and that, as long as that character is allowed it, it is to be handled with reverence, and studied with humility.

www.ingramcontent.com/pod-product-compliance
Lightning Source LLC
Chambersburg PA
CBHW070443090426
42735CB00012B/2450

* 9 7 8 1 6 0 6 0 8 9 2 0 0 *